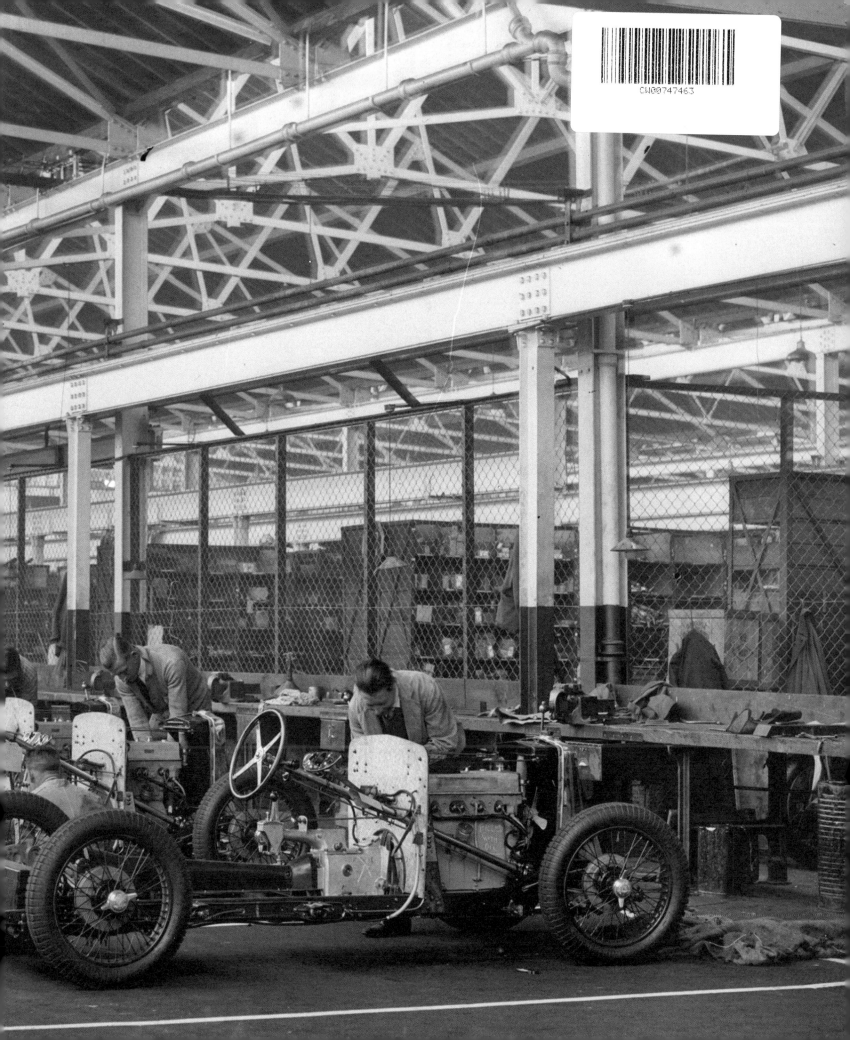

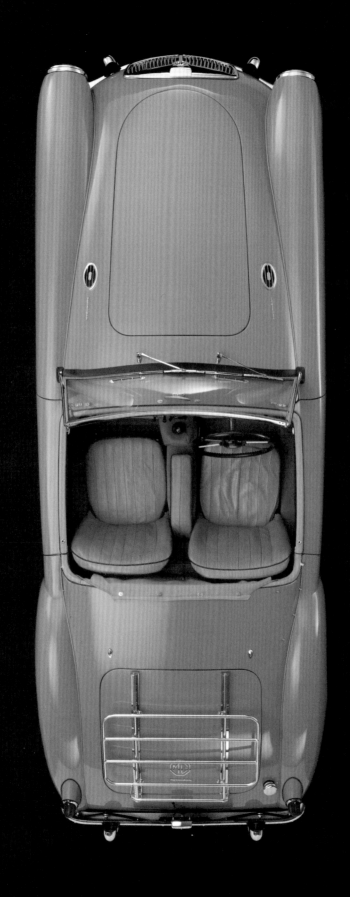

THE COMPLETE BOOK OF

CLASSIC MG CARS

ROSS ALKUREISHI

CONTENTS

From humble beginnings as an offshoot of Morris Motors Ltd., MG rose to become a marque in its own right. Imbued from the start with an impudent sporting prowess, its cars beguiled generation after generation of motoring enthusiast—both at home and around the world. Its famous octagonal badge in time became a guarantee of the quality, performance, and sheer character of its products.

Just as its inspired "Safety Fast!" marketing slogan suggested, right from the start MG tried to offer buyers a product that was one step up from the norm: highly attractive, well-engineered, and with a built in promise of swift, but supremely safe, motoring.

Initially a rebodied Morris Cowley, it quickly moved on to reengineering its donor parts, and then bespoke production. The arrival of the revolutionary M-Type Midget made sports car ownership affordable to the general public for the first time, and kickstarted a development space race.

During the 1930s, the MG name became synonymous with racing and speed-record-breaking successes, before new corporate ownership brought it to heel.

After World War II, MG was at the forefront of the export boom with model after model gaining the title of "world's bestselling sports car." Its inexpensive T-Type Midgets, MGA, MGB, and Midgets entranced buyers the world over.

It was by no means plain sailing, as multiple ownership changes saw it endure lean years and sometimes struggle for survival. Always, though, it continued to try to produce cars that adhered to its core values.

After the privations of the British Leyland years, MG endured to be revitalized in the 1990s with its innovative mid-engine MGF—once again, the octagon had a car worthy of the badge.

It all come crashing down in the new millennium, with the arrival and subsequent conduct of the Phoenix Group.

Yet the purpose of this book isn't to focus on tales of corporate mismanagement, but instead to celebrate the vintage, classic, and modern classic output of one of Britain's, and indeed the world's, finest sports car manufacturers.

IN THE BEGINNING THERE WAS MORRIS

In the very early part of the twentieth century, motoring was still principally a pursuit for those of significant means. However, by its second decade the times were changing quickly and a new guard of automobile producers, including the Ford Motor Company in North America and Morris Motors Ltd. in Great Britain, was busy targeting the high-volume, low-price market.

It was clear from a young age that William Richard Morris was destined to become an entrepreneur. Possessed both with a formidable character and a clear vision, he first began a bicycle repair business in a building at the bottom of the garden of his parents' home in James Street Cowley St John, an inner suburb of Oxford. This quickly expanded to include motorcycles and proper premises (including a showroom at 48 High Street, in the center of the city). By 1905 automobiles had joined the stable in the form of a motorcar hire and repair company and a taxi firm.

The move into automobile manufacturing was a natural one facilitated by the purchase, and conversion, of the derelict former Military Training College in Morris's hometown. There in 1913, under the banner of W.R.M Motors Ltd., he began constructing his first vehicle, the Morris Oxford.

This two-seater was built to Morris's own design but consisted of components almost entirely sourced from external suppliers, including its 1018cc four-cylinder, side-valve, 8.9-horsepower White & Poppe engine and three-speed gearbox. Its most distinctive feature though, sitting up front, was its cowled "bullnose" radiator; this endowed it with a rambunctious visual character, even if the performance reality was a touch more prosaic. However, keenly priced at £165 and with admirable build quality and equipment levels, the Oxford sold strongly from the start.

With a notable 353 examples finding buyers that first year, it was a very good start that its four-seat evolution, the 11.9-horsepower Cowley soon followed. This initial success proved that his new car did indeed have a market, but little could Morris have envisaged that he'd begun a journey that would lead to becoming one of the UK's leading industrialists and a multimillionaire, and with it, the title of Viscount Nuffield.

Little, too, could he have foreseen the pivotal role that its sister company, Morris Garages—formed to sell, service, and market the vehicles (alongside other marques)—would play in the future. While the Oxford became the bestselling car of the 1920s, with the now renamed Morris Motors Ltd. at one point holding a seismic 41 percent market share, in 1921 a catalyst for change arrived in the form of a certain Mr. Cecil Kimber.

The assembly line for the Morris Bullnose, Oxfordshire, 1925.

CHAPTER 1

MORRIS GARAGES TO MG:
FORMING, STORMING, NORMING, AND PERFORMING

The 1922 appointment of Cecil Kimber put Morris Garages on the road to forming MG as a distinct company. As its style evolved from the early special "Chummy" bodied cars, through the 11.9-horsepower Raworth Super Sports, to the "Bullnose" 14/28 MG Super Sports, including "Old Number One," it gained a reputation as a builder of quality, reliable, affordable, and thoroughly sporting wares.

The famous octagon makes an appearance on the early cars, but while the radiator badge states "M.G. Super Sports," in the center it's still branded "Morris Oxford."

1921–1923:
HUMBLE BEGINNINGS

Morris had never been an automobile manufacturer per se; his business model was instead to buy components from suppliers for his workers to use in constructing his Morris vehicles, and then in due course snap them up.

He'd already done that with engine builder Hotchkiss et Cie in May 1922, turning it into Morris Engines Ltd, and did so again with axle and chassis parts manufacturer E. G. Wrigley. It was there that he met Kimber and, recognizing the ambition that burned within the young man, in 1921 he brought him across to Morris Garages.

Morris continued to voraciously build his empire, gradually purchasing control of every aspect associated with production and maximizing profit every step of the way. Kimber, promoted to general manager in 1922, looked after the day-to-day running of the Oxford operation.

The 11 9 h p Morris-Cowley Occasional Four   Price £172 10s.
The 11 9 h p Morris-Cowley Occasional Four with four-wheel brakes   Price £180

Coachwork in grey or blue and upholstery to match.
Complete with full equipment, as specified, and one year's insurance (see page 8).

THE Occasional Four-seater Morris-Cowley fills the needs of the motorist who, while normally requiring only a two-seater car, desires occasionally to carry more than one passenger. Behind the two main seats of the Occasional Four are two folding seats, which provide ample accommodation for children or short-distance accommodation for adults. When folded, the space behind the rear seats is eminently suitable for carrying luggage, commercial traveller's samples, golf clubs, and other items that are normally out of place in the boot of a two-seater ; and one of the chief claims of the Occasional Four-seater or " Chummy " model, is that the space at the rear, whether it be occupied by passengers or packages—is under the hood in rainy weather, thus ensuring proper protection. This makes a big appeal to the man with a young family. Children, moreover, are safer in a " Chummy " model than they are in the dickey seat of a two-seater.

Side curtains are provided with the hood, the latter clipping down on to the windscreen supports to form a weather-tight joint between the front of the hood stick and the top of the windscreen. The side-panels can be left in position when the hood is down, if desired.

(Left) The yellow and black Raworth-bodied "M.G. Super Sports Morris" purchased by Oliver Arkell for £350.

(Opposite) A Morris-Cowley Occasional Four quickly replicated Kimber's successful design, prompting him to move on quickly.

This was a good grounding in all aspects of the business. He quickly learned customers' likes and dislikes, what worked and didn't work in terms of the products themselves, and most importantly what did and did not appeal.

Kimber's first steps at offering something a bit different involved the Morris Cowley. He bought them in bare chassis form and had them clothed in a specially devised body. Marketed at the start of 1923 as "The Morris Garages Chummy," up front it still featured the unmistakable Morris radiator (as featured on both Cowley and Oxford), but the four-seater looked distinctly sportier and a little less severe than its progenitor. In terms of mechanicals and running gear it was identical, with a Cowley 102-inch (259.1 cm) chassis, 11.9-horsepower engine, three-speed nonsynchromesh gearbox, half-elliptic leaf spring front suspension, quarter-elliptic rear suspension, drum brakes, and 4.75:1 spiral bevel final drive. It came as standard in Pastel Blue, although other colors could be had for an additional £5, and featured a leather interior.

The Chummy allowed a family of four to travel under the same roof rather than with some in a rumble seat. He sold an impressive 109 examples. Unsurprisingly Morris Motors introduced its own Occasional-4 for the 1924 model, undercutting Kimber's Chummy by quite a margin; undaunted, Kimber turned his attention to a new two-seat body for the 11.9-horsepower Cowley chassis, commissioning Oxford coachbuilder Raworth to build six open-top bodies.

The resulting Raworth Super Sport was far more than a rebodied Morris. It was now capable of 60 miles per hour, and new steering and springing improved handling. Features such as swept wings, scuttle ventilators, and a windshield with triangulated end piers went on to become iconic MG features. And there was no doubting Kimber's eye for a line, as the re-bodied car had a dynamic and rakish look.

CECIL KIMBER:
FATHER OF THE MARQUE

Having attended the Stockport Grammar and Manchester Technical Schools, Kimber then joined his father's printing ink business at the age of sixteen. During his apprenticeship he was involved in a serious road accident while riding his 1906 motorcycle.

A considerable recovery time and a permanent limp from the incident did little to temper his considerable passion for motoring, other than to switch his loyalties from two wheels to four: a Singer 10 that he bought with his compensation money.

Determined to gain a job in the still fledgling motor industry, but with as yet undeveloped technical knowledge, he gained employment at Sheffield-based carmaker Sheffield-Simplex, then moved to AC Cars in Thames Ditton. Another switch to Birmingham-based axle and chassis parts builder E. G. Wrigley followed, this time as works manager.

In 1921 his infectious, energetic, and positive personality impressed Morris. Kimber took his skills to the Morris Garages at Oxford, initially as sales manager, but quickly progressing to general manager.

After realizing that modification of existing output could raise profit margins, he began producing bespoke bodywork for Morris models. This quickly grew to include mechanical upgrades, and very soon the MG marque was born.

Though Kimber continued to nurture and guide it through challenging economic times and ownership changes, he found himself unemployed in 1941. Morris, by now Viscount Nuffield, was reportedly unimpressed by his conduct in both his private life and in the workplace.

Kimber gained another position at a London engineering company in 1942. But, just over two years later, after failing to secure the petrol coupons needed to drive his MG to a sales meeting in Peterborough, he was tragically killed in a freak railway accident at Kings Cross station on Sunday, February 4, 1945.

Oliver Arkell took delivery of the first example, with yellow body and black wings, on August 11, 1923, but the last of these—significantly more expensive at £350 than the mechanically identical Cowley two-seater at £195— took until well into the new year to find a home.

1924–1925: MORRIS OR MG, MG OR MORRIS?

Neither quite one thing nor another, Kimber's sideline still sat firmly in the middle. His first two offerings had shown he was on to something. Was it simply the visual tweaking of Morris models, or did it have designs on being more?

With the horrors of the First World War now a distant memory, and the economy booming, car ownership was on the up and motor sport—from trialing to newly formed blue-ribbon race events, such as Le Mans—was now in the ascendency.

British manufacturer Bentley already occupied the upper echelons of this change, although not yet dominating it. It finished fourth at the 1923 24 Hours of Le Mans, but victory came the following year with a 3 Litre Sport.

Bentley's products, aimed firmly at society's elite, were clearly bathing in the reflective glow of success. Surely something similar could be achieved more affordably.

In 1924 the Morris chassis received the up-rated 13.9 horsepower 1,802.5cc engine. This period was the turning point for the fledging concern. Not only did it re-clothe the new chassis with an attractive, alloy-paneled body, it began to make chassis and running gear changes to improve performance. As such, suspension springs were flattened (with Hartford shock absorbers fitted at the rear and Gabriel snubbers at the front), steering columns lowered, and engines modified.

Designed by Kimber's cost accountant, Ted Lee, the famed octagonal MG (an acronym for Morris Garages,

Note the MG-style triangular glass framed windscreen and raked steering wheel in this photo of what was probably the first 1924 short-wheelbase Super Sports.

(Above) Built in January 1925, this four-seater 14/28 Super Sports is the earliest surviving MG.

(Opposite bottom) As this early ad shows, the new 14/28 Super Sports could be had in both the rakish two-seater and larger four-seater forms at a cost of £345 for the former and £360 for the latter.

(Opposite top) The Chummy bodied Morris, so-called because the rear occupants sat facing each other in side-mounted seats and the top could cover all four occupants.

naturally) badge appeared on cars (on their door thresh-old plates) for the first time this year, although it had already appeared in advertisements the previous year.

Just to confuse matters, they named the new model the 14/28 Super Sports MG Four-Door Saloon Morris Oxford. The newcomer was striding forward, but still wasn't quite ready to throw off its master's shackles.

It was certainly pricier than the Morris Oxford, but not as expensive as the public had come to expect of a sporting car. As you'd expect of an affordable car that had the possibility of transforming the landscape (and thus drawing more people in to motoring in all its forms), Kimber's wares found an early proponent in *Motor Sport*, which carried out its first road test in October 1925. The magazine reported that, on arrival, MG engineers stripped down the standard Morris engine, balanced its moving components, and cleaned and polished the ports before reassembly and bench check.

The magazine recorded a top speed of 65 miles per hour and praised both the updated looks (particularly with reference to the flowing mudguards and Ace wheel discs) and lively performance with 0 to 50 miles per hour taking just over 24 seconds. The only caution referenced the belligerent exhaust note, criticized as being most likely to attract police attention (something that sports car fans happily paid extra for in the many decades that followed!).

Being based on the Morris Oxford was a blessing. Morris was the fastest-selling car in Great Britain, eclipsing both Ford and Austin. This heritage endowed the MG with Morris reliability and allowed it to be sold with a Morris guarantee.

Knowing now that Kimber's tuning methods would help aid sales without compromising reliability—or invoking claims—Morris overcame his initial reticence about allowing Kimber to modify the engines. The simple modifications ensured that an engine that already produced 32 brake horsepower in standard form now had an output in the region of 40 brake horsepower.

(Above) Regular competitor Russell Chiesman overtakes a stranded Bugatti on Porlock Hill in his 14/28 Super Sports, during the 1926 Land's End Trial.

(Right) This 1927 two-seater 14/28 Super Sports is endowed with the new "Flatnose" radiator, which was both more efficient and cheaper to produce.

(Opposite) Pictured in a scrapyard in the 1930s, this is a smaller two-seater 14/28 Super Sports.

Thanks to a special MG bracket, a key feature of the new model was a steering column with a new low rake, set at 25 degrees off the horizontal as compared to the 45 degrees off the horizontal "sit-up-and-beg" unit of the Bullnose Morris car. This allowed the car to be fitted with lower, sportier coachwork.

The MG from Morris Garages was gaining a reputation as a blooming' quick and capable performer, and one that looked good to boot. For a general public used to sports cars being the sole preserve of the well-to-do, they were absolute manna from heaven, and production was quickly ramped up to meet demand.

1926: END OF AN ERA

Further versions of the 14/28 followed, including a £345 two-seater roadster, a saloon, and even a Landaulet. When the 6-inch (15.2 cm) longer Oxford chassis with better brakes arrived, production switched to this. By 1926 nearly 400 "Bullnose" MGs were sold. Kimber's endeavor rapidly grew from being merely tolerated to being a genuine and impressive business concern.

He'd well and truly caught the imagination of the up-and-coming middle classes. In the next decade and a half, his recipe for more desirable, better looking, and hotter specification sports cars (all based on more humble underpinnings) really took off.

However, like in all businesses, going forwards sometimes meant having to go back. In this case, the cause was the arrival of the radically revised Morris Oxford. Gone was the character-defining bulbous snout that had endowed every Oxford/Cowley since 1913 with their equally memorable "Bullnose" sobriquet, replaced by a decidedly undistinguished (although certainly more efficient) "Flatnose." Worse still, the new chassis frame—while wider and stronger—was also heavier. With no changes to the engine, performance inevitably took a hit.

Note the missing rear offside mudguard in this post-Trial shot of the victorious Kimber.

OLD NUMBER ONE: (NOT QUITE) THE FIRST MG

The MG (originally M.G.) marque's genesis was a symbiotic one, growing initially from one man's ideas and evolving for a number of years. It eventually separated (never entirely) from its Morris origins to become a concrete concept.

As such, its beginnings aren't quite as clear cut as those of other automobile makes. Old Number One (as it was later called), described by Kimber in 1931 as ". . . the forerunner of the present MG car," and which he suggested in 1937 could ". . . justly be termed No. 1 MG," wasn't the very first.

It can, though, lay claim to being the first MG purpose-built for competition. Kimber took a gold medal on the Motor Cycling Club's 1923 Land's End Trial, in a mildly modified

(flattened springs and a raised engine compression ratio, among others) Chummy. The resultant publicity had a small but noticeable effect on sales, so in his mind it made sense to commission a vehicle from his now fledgling brand in which to attack the 1925 event.

Based on a modified "Bullnose" Morris Cowley chassis (with hand-forged side rails that curved over the rear axle), it featured a bespoke lightweight body by Carbodies of Coventry and a 1,548cc, four-cylinder, Hotchkiss engine from a Scottish Glichrist car with a special overhead valve cylinder head design. Tuned to give around 25 brake horsepower (by machining and polishing the head and modifying the carburetor), it was allied to a standard three-speed Morris transmission, while special half-elliptic springs were fitted at the rear. Finally they lowered the steering column, fitted tall wire-spoke wheels, and fitted two small lights on either side of the scuttle.

Registered FC 7900 on March 27 and raced in Battleship Grey, the vehicle gained Kimber his second gold medal in the Light Car class. The sight of his dynamic, bulbous-nosed MG special powering nobly up one gravel-tracked hill after another, and onwards to motor sport success, was exactly the association Kimber wanted the public to make when hearing the letters M and G.

"Old Number One" caused a controversy when it competed in the up to 1,500cc class at the Trial with a 1,548cc engine. Told it would be moved up to the next class, Kimber denied the car was over 1,500cc and was allowed to keep his award!

Kimber climbed the Blue Mines section of the 1925 Land's End Trial in his special "Old Number One." Found languishing in a scrap yard during the 1930s, it was bought by MG, restored, painted red, and subsequently used for publicity.

The new sober-suited 14/28 hit both lower visual and performance heights than its predecessor. It was the automotive equivalent of a seeing a bon viveur in full flow one night, and then again the following, having giving up the good stuff for religious reasons.

There was only one thing to do. Marles Weller steering replaced the Morris setup, Hartford shock absorbers replaced the Smiths dampers, and the team reworked the braking layout, added wire spoke wheels fitted with balloon-type tires (rather than bead-edge types), restyled the body, and, most importantly, stripped the engine and gave it a thorough reworking.

Relaunched as the 14/40 (it later gained an MG MkIV designation) at the London Motor Show, it was the first to sport the chocolate-and-cream octagon on its radiator badge and had regained the lost performance ground thanks to a marginally higher power output.

As successful as these early cars were, Kimber had exciting plans for the marque. Far from simply modifying existing Morris cars, he had a different vision. And for that it was time for some new models.

(Top) The famous "Old Speckled Hen," an MG Featherlight Saloon covered with a synthetic leather-look fabric that would become a factory runabout.

(Above) The magnificent 14/40 Super Sports in all its glory was the first model of MG as a marque in its own right. Its chassis and guarantee plates were issued by Morris Garages rather than Morris Motors.

1923

Super Sports, Raworth Two-Seater

Models	Two-seater Roadster (£350)	Gearbox	3-speed manual
Construction	Steel channel-section chassis frame, steel body panels on a wooden bodyshell skeleton	Automatic	n/a
		Final Drive Ratio	4.75:1
Length	n/a	Steering	Worm and wheel
Width	n/a	Front Suspension	Beam axle, half-elliptic leaf springs
Height	n/a	Rear Suspension	Live (beam) axle on three-quarter elliptic leaf springs, optional Gabriel snubbers
Wheelbase	102 in (259.1 cm)		
Weight	n/a	Tires	700 × 80 Dunlop Cord beaded-edge tires
Engine Size	1,548cc		
Engine Format	In-line 4-cylinder	Brakes	9-in (22.9 cm) drums (front)
Carburetion	1 × Solex 1.3 in (30 mm)	0 to 50 mph	n/a
Max Bhp	26 bhp @ 2,800 rpm	Top Speed	65 mph (104.6 km/h)
Max Torque	n/a	Fuel Economy	19 mpg (US, 15.82 mpg)

1924–1926

As above for MG Super Sports 14/28 "Bullnose" except

Models	Two-seater Roadster (£350), Open four-seater Roadster (£375), Salonette Two-seater (£475), Salonette Four-seater (£495)	Max Bhp	40 bhp @ 4,000 rpm (est)
		Front Suspension	Beam axle, half-elliptic leaf springs, Gabriel snubbers
		Rear Suspension	Live (beam) axle on three-quarter elliptic leaf springs, Hartford shock absorbers (Duplex Hartfords on Salonette)
Length	152 in (386.1 cm)		
Width	60 in (152.4 cm)		
Height	65 in (165.1 cm)	Tires	28 × 4.95 Dunlop reinforced balloon tires
Engine Size	1,802cc		
Carburetion	1 × Smith, Solex, or SU	0 to 50 mph	23.8 sec

1926–1929

MG Super Sports, 14/28 "Flatnose," and 14/40 (MkIV)

Models	Two-seater Roadster (£340), Four-seater Roadster (£350), Salonette Two-seater (£475), Four-seater (£475), MkIV Sports Salonette (£445)	Max Torque	n/a
		Gearbox	3-speed manual
		Automatic	n/a
Construction	Steel channel-section chassis frame, alloy body panels on a wooden bodyshell skeleton	Final Drive Ratio	4.42:1
		Steering	Worm and wheel
		Front Suspension	Beam axle, half-elliptic leaf springs, Smith rebound shock absorbers
Length	150 in (381 cm)		
Width	61 in (154.94 cm)	Rear Suspension	Live (beam) axle on half-elliptic leaf springs, Hartford shock absorbers
Height	n/a		
Wheelbase	106.5 in (270.5 cm)	Tires	28 in × 4.95 in
Weight	1,764 lb (800.1 kg), chassis only	Brakes	12-in (30.5 cm) drums, front and rear, servo assistance
Engine Size	1,802cc		
Engine Format	In-line 4-cylinder	0 to 60 mph	n/a
Carburetion	1 × Solex 1.3 in (30 mm)	Top Speed	67 mph (107.8 km/h)
Max Bhp	40 bhp @ 4,000 rpm (est)	Fuel Economy	28 mpg (US, 24.6 mpg)

CHAPTER 2

IN ITS OWN RIGHT

With the line between Morris and MG vehicles widening, the latter finally became a company in its own right and moved to new premises. However, the launch of its new 18/80 came at exactly the wrong time, as the New York stock market crashed in 1929. Luckily a second new car, the M-Type Midget, saved the day. The rest of the decade was a whirlwind of motorsport success, before it all came to an abrupt halt.

The MG M-Type Midget of C.J. Randall and F.M Montgomery battles that of H.H. Stisted and Norman Black at the Brooklands track, on Friday, May 9, 1930.

The M.G. Car Company

(Proprietors: The Morris Garages Ltd.)

Telephone: Oxford 2241

Telegrams: "Emgee, Oxford"

Queen Street

MG

Oxford

Governing Director: W. R. Morris

General Manager: Cecil Kimber

M.G. Service Depot Telephone . . . . Cowley 7000

December, 1928.

TO ALL MOTOR TRADERS.

Dear Sirs,

All M.G. Sports Cars are designed and produced by specialists in the manufacture of Sports Cars. They are assembled in the M.G. model factory at Oxford which is devoted exclusively to this purpose.

The engines—which are built in Europe's finest engine factory—and most of the components, are special and exclusive to the M.G. Sports Car. Each car is treated individually from the start, and an extraordinarily high standard of efficiency is thus obtained. This results in an almost total lack of after-sales service required and thereby the conservation of your profit.

Judging by certain articles concerning M.G. Sports Cars which have recently appeared in the press, it seems that those responsible still do not appreciate the fact that M.G. Sports Cars are an entirely distinct production. In order to remove any doubt from the minds of British Motor Traders we repeat that M.G. Sports Cars are not ''hotted up'' or sports editions of any standard car, but are designed and built in every detail as Sports Cars and represent the entire output of the factory.

We should appreciate the opportunity of showing you round the M.G. works.

Yours very truly,

THE M.G. CAR COMPANY.

Cecil Kimber

General Manager.

Morris formally acknowledged the new marque's success by registering The MG Car Company Limited (proprietors The Morris Garages Limited) in March 1928. It was a vindication of Kimber's brainchild and his team's hard work, but most telling was the section in parentheses, which left no one in doubt as to who still owned the new concern.

Kimber was likely too busy forging on with his ambitious plans to have had the discussion with the famously parsimonious Morris as to an ownership stake (even if he had, it'd probably have been unsuccessful—another famously tried similar later, to no avail). However, like workers the world over (no matter how lofty their position in a company), it left him vulnerable—employees after all, could always be replaced.

In its first statement of both independence and intent, MG presented the 18/80 at the October 1928 Olympia Motor Show. The model marked a step upmarket, with its 2.5-liter overhead camshaft engine (naturally adapted with a stronger cylinder block and four-main-

bearing crankshaft, twin SU carburetors, and 60 brake horsepower) based on that of the Morris Six. However, very little of that car remained, as Kimber had been given the go-ahead to design an entirely new, strong, and lower chassis frame. Accordingly, the suspension and steering had been reworked for a sportier driving experience. As per previous models it featured a fresh body, but the biggest change was a first appearance for the distinctive new Kimber-designed radiator. This vertical unit dominated its façade and was crowned with the octagonal MG badge. For those that viewed it on the Motor Show stand, there was no doubt that memories of Morris were fast receding.

Those admiring it also noted a cheeky, diminutive prototype junior partner sitting next to it. The family resemblance of the M-Type Midget was clear, thanks to a matching radiator, but this wisp of a car was a veritable flyweight compared to its heavyweight big brother.

Again, with newfound freedoms Kimber got the okay to look elsewhere in the Morris empire for engines and

(Above) This photo shows just
how much presence the 18/80
Speed model had.

(Opposite) The 1930 and 1931
model line-up had something
for everyone.

running gear. With one eye on Austin's 7, he based this
secondary new model on the new Morris Minor. Unlike
the 18/80, the Midget was built down to a cost; there was
no fancy new chassis, just a fresh, lightweight two-seater
fabric body set straight down on the existing frame. Under
the hood sat the tiny Morris Minor 847cc four-cylinder
overhead-camshaft engine from the sedan. Despite being
small in capacity, this Wolseley-designed engine (Wolseley also having been consumed by the Morris empire in
1927) was a sophisticated and vigorous little unit.

Best of all, Kimber pitched this entry-level model
to sell at a scandalously low £175 and instantly made
sports car hijinks affordable for the burgeoning middle
classes. Compare that to the £485 asking price for the
18/80, which with its "junior" Bentley aspirations was
in an entirely different fiscal league.

With its opening statement made as a company now
in its own right, MG had to sit back and wait to see how
the public and press reacted to its new wares.

1928–1930: MG

Prior to the show, in an article titled "A Six-Cylinder MG—Sports Car with Many Interesting Mechanical Features," *The Autocar* stated of the 18/80, "The new car is a great improvement on the old one, is beautifully sprung, holds the road well, has very powerful brakes and, by reason of the six-cylinder engine, is quiet and very smooth".

Starting with praise was a good step, but the crash of the New York Stock Exchange, and its subsequent worldwide economic repercussions, was a disaster for a car priced at the 18/80's level (the sedan was even higher at £525). It wouldn't sell in great numbers.

The M-Type Midget by comparison had appeared at exactly the right time—its entry price point, a bargain prior to the market crash, actually benefited from the oncoming downturn.

Despite a relatively paltry 20 brake horsepower, with a curb weight of just 1,279 pounds (580 kg), it went like stink—or more importantly, it *felt* like it did. Throw in the engine's lovely, free-revving nature and devilish handling, and the plaudits were instant. In its June 1929 road test, titled "No 61. MG Midget Two-Seater—An Extraordinarily Fascinating Little Car: Comfort at Speed," *The Autocar* vociferously praised all aspects of the new car: ". . . it goes exceedingly well."; "In confined spaces the Midget is very easy to [maneuver], for the steering is light and quick, and one can twist and turn rapidly through traffic."; and, "It is perhaps in the hills that this infant phenomenon really excels," were just a few of the compliments (others being modern looks, fuel economy—38 mpg!—and engine and braking responses). The following month *Motor* concurred: ". . . the MG Midget fills a real niche in the sports car world, and is capable of holding its own with any other cars of similar type, whether of British or foreign origin. It is one of the most fascinating little vehicles we've ever driven."

The M-Type Midget was a true game-changer, bringing sports car motoring to an entirely new market.

LOCATION, LOCATION, LOCATION

The team constructed Kimber's trials special "Old Number One" in a tight corner of the Morris Garages premises at Longwall Street, Oxford. But his "Chummy" project required more space.

Morris rented another small premises in Alfred Lane for the purpose, but demand continued to grow. In 1925, Kimber arranged for the use of part of the Morris Motors Radiator factory building in Bainton Road, Oxford. Located close to the main Morris Motors assembly plant, the facility housed the growing concern until its purpose-built factory in Edmund Road, Cowley, was built (at a cost of £20,000).

But the unexpected torrent of M-Type Midget sales overwhelmed even the larger Cowley-based facility. In September 1929, MG moved to the site of the former Pavlova Leather Company (which had been a key supplier to the military during World War I, before going bust) in Abingdon. Seven miles south of Oxford, this quiet Thames-side town remained the company's base for half a century.

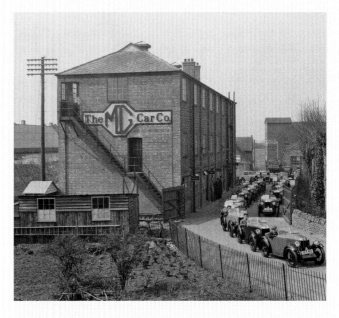

Brand new trade plate-wearing M-Type Midgets prepare to leave the MG Car Company's new Abingdon factory in 1930.

The public was quick to agree. Response to the new car was so swift that it soon necessitated another move to new premises for MG.

While the M-Type Midget (also available in sedan form) set the company's sports car template—simple ladder-type chassis, beam front and rear axles, vertical MG radiator, bench seat with central gear change, and exposed headlamps—development of the 18/80 continued for the next twenty-five years. In 1929, MG introduced the new MkII, with its stiffer frame, bigger 12-inch (30.5 cm) brakes, and new four-speed gearbox endowing it with longer legs.

An 18/100 MG Six MkIII road-racing variant, nicknamed "the Tigresse," followed in 1930. MG produced this no expense spared, comprehensively reengineered car, with its power output of 85 brake horsepower, in four-seater touring form only (unlike the standard 18/80, which by now could be bought with twelve different body styles). Unfortunately, in its first race outing, at that year's Brooklands Double Twelve Motorsport Festival, a carburetor butterfly came loose and was drawn into the engine, resulting in its failure. Despite this it was an immensely capable machine, and a very controllable high-speed warrior, but it was damned by both its 2,468cc engine capacity—which left it smack in the middle of its competition class (and unable to compete with the Bentleys and their ilk)—and an enormous £895 price tag. MG built just five. Meanwhile, at that same Brooklands race, the M-Type Midget did rather better...

The M-Type Midget had proven itself a sharp little performer on the Land's End Trials (with two gold and two silver medals in the 1929 running), a strong class

(Above) The 18/100 MkIII Tigress was a powerhouse of a car with an 85-bhp engine, but it was, by MG standards, also very expensive. They built just five, two of which survive to this day, including this example.

(Opposite) *Autocar* resident artist Frederick Gordon Crosby produced this invigorating illustration of a Brooklands Double-Twelve 18/100 Tigress, but it would be its smaller sibling that excelled there.

F. Gordon Crosby

finish on the 1930 Monte Carlo Rally, and the 1100cc record in the Mont des Mules hill climb.

Chief designer H. N. Charles had designed a new camshaft and upped power to 27 brake horsepower, and Midgets (relatively standard in spec, save minor mechanical tweaks but featuring Brooklands–type competition exhaust, a larger fuel tank, an exterior mounted spare wheel on the body side, and hood straps) finished third, fourth, fifth, sixth, and seventh in class at the 1930 Brooklands Double Twelve. In surely one of Great Britain's first examples of "race on a Sunday, sell on a Monday," twenty-one replica "Double Twelve" Midgets with fetching brown and cream coachwork were quickly constructed and sold to the public.

Come 1931, Kimber had a prototype chassis (the lower chassis as used in EX120) for a new C-Type racing derivative (just forty-four were built) of the M-Type Midget. The only trouble was, this time he'd committed to preparing fourteen cars. With that year's running of the "Double Twelve" race only eight weeks away, the factory had to move very quickly to meet this commitment.

The workforce's efforts were well worth it as the "new" C-Type Montlhéry (the name quickly adopted after testing at the French track) Midgets proved an unstoppable force, taking the first five places. The winning car, driven by The Earl of March and Chris Staniland, averaged an

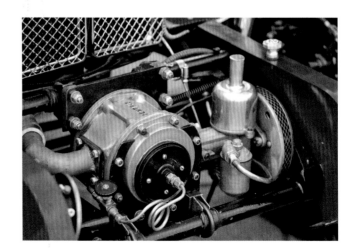

impressive 65.2 miles per hour (105.6 km/h). If the previous result had announced the Midget's arrival as contender on the national racing scene, then this one cemented its place as a winner. From a racing perspective MG's decade was just getting going, and things were only going to get better.

That same year Midgets achieved a 1-2-3 in the Saorstát Cup Race and were victorious in both the Irish Grand Prix and Ulster Tourist Trophy—a tremendous start for the newcomer.

A more incredible feat followed in 1933 when the supercharged C-Type Montlhéry Midget of John Ludovic Ford and Maurice Baumer won its class at the 24 Hours of Le Mans, finishing in sixth place overall (the smallest capacity car to ever finish so high) and second in the Index of Performance.

(Below) Sadly, the superbly crafted MG brackets on an 18/80 MkII chassis are usually covered by bodywork.

(Opposite top) The C-Type Midget retailed for £295 in standard form or £345 for a supercharged example. MG reduced engine capacity to 746cc in order to allow it to compete in the up to 750cc racing class.

(Opposite bottom) The supercharger sits up front and helps the C-Type produce 52.5 bhp (15.1 bhp more than the standard C-Type).

George Eyston drives "The Magic Midget" onto Pendine Sands, Carmarthenshire, on February 8, 1932, prior to breaking the World's Light Car Speed Record.

The 1930s were a scintillating era with regards to record attempts, and with Kimber's can-do motorsport outlook, it came as no surprise when MG entered that world.

EX120, a prototype C-Type racing car, featured an experimental low-slung chassis frame (main members were set parallel to each other, passing under the rear axle with tubular members linking the side frames) that became the basis for all MG chassis design over the next few decades. The team adapted it for Captain George Eyston, with a view to attacking the International Class H category and becoming the first 750cc–engined car to hit 100 mph.

Reducing stroke from 3.3 inches (83 mm) to 3.2 inches (81 mm) using a special counterbalanced crankshaft and reducing bore size by means of liners from 2.2 inches (57 mm) to 2.1 inches (54 mm), they reduced the standard engine's capacity to within limits at 742cc.

After a number of near misses trying to reach the magic number, Eyston had a Powerplus supercharger fitted, and in early 1931 at the banked Montlhéry track, just south of Paris, he finally triumphed, breaking the 5-kilometer record (among others) at a staggering 103.13 mph (166 km/h).

He'd return in December, this time to try and become the first 750cc car to cover 100 miles in the hour. This he did, averaging 101.01 miles per hour, but on an extra lap EX120 caught fire with Eyston suffering serious, but non–life–threatening, burns.

The publicity resulting from having achieved the feat before rival company Austin (its 7 had come agonizingly short at 97 mph in late 1930) merely added to a burgeoning MG legend. This was the first of numerous experimental MG record cars, and the redoubtable Eyston returned to pilot EX127 in 1932.

The "Magic Midget" had a C-Type chassis with an offset driveline that allowed the driver to sit lower in the cockpit. The team fitted it with an aerodynamic Reg Jackson–designed body (tested in the Vickers wind tunnel at Brooklands), and its 745cc supercharged engine produced a fearsome 98 brake horsepower. After his last EX120 experience, Eyston wore protective asbestos overalls as he set four speed records at 114.77 miles per hour (184.7 km/h).

A failed attempt to take the two-miles-per-minute record at Pendine Sands followed, but he finally achieved it (once more at Montlhéry) in December that same year with a speed of over 120.56 miles per hour (193 km/h), thereby taking the mile and kilometer records.

1931–1932:
THE NEXT GENERATION

MG entered a hyperactive period of continual improvement and redevelopment of both road and race cars, in which it designated almost every letter of the alphabet to a model.

First up was the spin-off D-Type Midget, the first production model to use the new C-Type chassis. This was in essence a midi-Midget, as it lengthened the wheelbase from the original's 6 feet 9 inches (2 m) to 7 feet (2.1 m) and then again to 7 feet 2 inches (2.2 m), which allowed the fitment of four-seater bodywork (both open and closed). But it was bigger and heavier, and as the M-Type engine remained the same, it took a bit of a performance hit.

Despite his previous six-cylinder experiences, Kimber forged ahead with a new model: the F-Type Magna. Using the 1,271cc six-cylinder from the Wolseley Hornet (somewhat cheekily MG tried to

(Above) In January 1934, chassis fettling at the MG Motorworks in Abingdon.

(Right) This study from the September 11, 1930, issue of *Autocar* shows the underlying mechanical structure, including the six-cylinder engine and four-speed gearbox.

The Magnette K1 **Saloon de Luxe**

A striking red K1 Magnette Saloon de Luxe in its natural habitat features in this 1930s advertisement.

The team removes the dustcovers and readies the F-Type Magna and J-Type Midget for the Olympia Motor Show in London.

hide its humbler origins with sheet-metal panels), this car was essentially a six-cylinder version of the Midget and had a 73-mile-per-hour top speed. It proved more successful than its predecessors, selling 1,250 total examples of all variants.

Motor Sport called it "…a very attractive high performance car, with a special appeal to the man who has to consider reliability and economy, and yet desires a car with individuality." As the recession bit deeper, MG's reputation continued to grow. At £250 for the open sports or £289 for the very funky-looking Closed Salonette, it tempted some owners of bigger and more expensive cars to downsize, while those Midget owners that lusted after something larger could aspire to owning one.

The original M-Type Midget bowed out in June 1932, having sold a preposterous 3,235 examples, making it

without doubt the world's favorite sports car. In came its replacement: the J-Type Midget, a mixture of the old and the new. It had the same D-Type chassis and axles, and even the engine was the same 847cc unit. However, engineers endowed the latter with a crossflow cylinder head and twin SU carburetors for a decidedly perky 36 brake horsepower at 5,500 rpm, and it was the first Midget endowed with a four-speed gearbox. Sold in J1 (four–seater open or closed) and J2 (two-seater sports) forms, it was joined in 1933 by J3 and J4 racing variants.

That would have been enough for most established companies, never mind a still embryonic concern, but, to assist Kimber's desire to compete in the 1,100cc Class G category (midway between Midget and Magna), MG launched yet another six-cylinder car: the K-Series Magnette. To be sold in K1 (four-seater open or four-seat sedan), K2 (two-seater sports), and again later in 1933 K3 (race car) variants, this used the by now tried-and-true MG chassis design but of a much more substantial construction (and in two lengths: one for the smaller two-seat cars and a longer one for the four-seaters). It now had 13-inch brake drums, an engine designed purely for MG use and a Wilson pre-selector gearbox.

Although nominally based on the F-Types, the new engine had been redesigned, modified, and strengthened, gaining a new crossflow cylinder head design, and some versions were equipped with triple SU carburetors. Though smaller in capacity, it was more powerful. How much, exactly (39 to 48.5 brake horsepower), depended on the engine chosen, as there were three variants: KA, KB, and KD (four if the later K3 is included).

To confuse matters, there were also three chassis, three gearboxes, and five body types. K-Series Magnettes sold in very small numbers and didn't prove hugely popular (customers complained of the early KA-engined examples being underpowered). Unsurprisingly, given the sheer number of variables, no two cars were quite the same.

The K3 Magnette race car fared rather better.

1933: MOTORSPORT PINNACLE

If MG's earlier attempt to mix it up with the big boys had been a nonstarter, going toe-to-toe with Maserati and Alfa Romeo on their home turf, and putting them to the sword, announced the marque's arrival as a serious contender on the international stage.

The model that did so was the supercharged 1,086cc, six-cylinder K3 Magnette, with its specially made chassis, modified C-Type racing body, and 120-brake horsepower output, of which just thirty-three examples were built between 1933 and 1934. The most famous of these, and without doubt one of the most illustrious MGs of all, was K3003.

As part of a three-car team, it entered the 1933 Mille Miglia. MG had done its homework, sending a prerace team to test in Italy and identifying weaknesses (the front axle

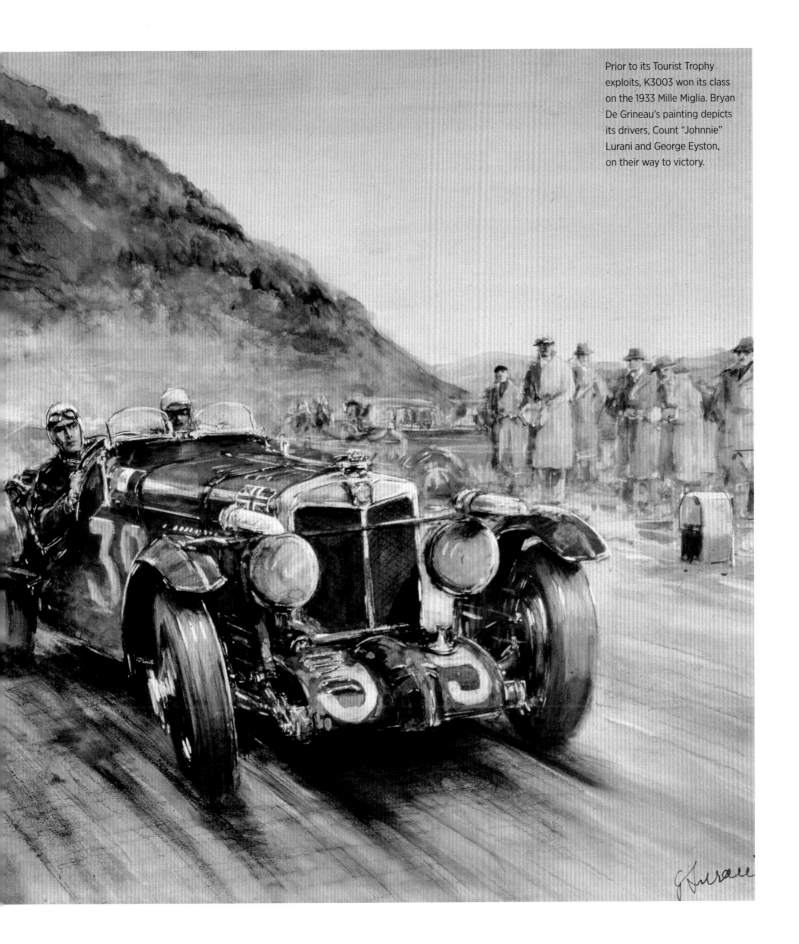

Prior to its Tourist Trophy exploits, K3003 won its class on the 1933 Mille Miglia. Bryan De Grineau's painting depicts its drivers, Count "Johnnie" Lurani and George Eyston, on their way to victory.

among them) that required strengthening before the event proper.

From the start of the race, Sir Henry Birkin and Bernard Rubin set a ferocious pace in their K3, forcing the works Maseratis to follow suit and ultimately suffer mechanical failure. Valve trouble forced the hard-worked Birkin/Rubin car to retire, but not without leaving the way open for George Eyston and Count "Johnnie" Lurani to power to victory in K3003. Earl Howe and "Hammy" Hamilton finished second in the other K3. As a result, MG also took the coveted team prize, with the winning car demolishing existing 1,100cc-class records.

This was the provenance that the Eyston/Lurani car had before Kimber offered it to one of the world's most formidable racing drivers, Tazio Nuvolari, for that year's Ulster Tourist Trophy race.

With MG development engineer Alec Hounslow as his co-driver, Nuvolari in his trademark flat-out, side-ways-sliding style broke the 1,100cc lap record seven times and astoundingly won the entire event on a handicap.

Other K3 Magnettes went on to great things, including Charles Martin and Roy Eccles's victory in the 2.0-liter class (and fourth overall) at the 1935 24 Hours of Le Mans.

But it was the Nuvolari car that a whole generation of schoolboys grew up revering.

In autumn 1933 the J-Series Midgets received a styling update, with new graceful swept front fenders replacing the old cycle types. That same year the supercharged J3 road-racing and J4 race car variants were made available.

In fact, Hugh Hamilton's J4 (chassis number J4002) had finished second to the Nuvolari car at the TT. Due to its high power output of 72.3 brake horsepower it was a particularly hairy car to pilot. It ran close to the limits of the chassis, with 12-inch (30.5 cm) drum brakes not in the same class as the speed developed.

Those brakes came from the new L-Type Magna, which had replaced the F-Type. At this point MG was guilty of a bit of mix 'n' match when it came to chassis, engines, and bodies. However, the L-Type, with its 1,087cc twin SU-fed six-cylinder engine developing a smooth 41 brake horsepower, was a nice combination of engineering and styling; sold in L1 four-seater and L2 two-seater open styles, it was well-liked and sold accordingly.

The life cycle of MG models was particularly short, which didn't bode well from an economic perspective. It was clear that problems were brewing. Despite the continuing high-level Midget sales, the factory had been in the red in both 1931 and 1933. A combination of constant innovation and reinvention, coupled with the high costs of motorsport involvement, did its best to negate profits.

Yet again, it'd be all change for 1934.

1934–1935: REALITY BITES

Hubert Charles and his team (which now included a young man named Syd Enever) fully reengineered the new P-Type Midget to have a sturdier chassis and stronger three-main-bearing crankshaft engine. Some of the earliest J-Series models' two-bearing units had suffered failures, due to their lofty power outputs. It came with 12-inch (30.5 cm) drum brakes (all predecessors had 8-inch [20.3 cm] drums), and Charles's team

strengthened its gearbox and rear axle. Best of all was Kimber's new styling, which demonstrated he hadn't lost his eye for an endearing design. It was sold as a two-seater sports model, a four-seater, and in (wildly aerodynamic) Airline Coupe form.

MG released another new model at the same time: the N-Type Magnette (and from mid–1934, longer-chassis KN Magnette) rationalized the six-cylinder models by replacing both the Magna and K Magnettes. The 1,271cc six-cylinder unit had been improved with a crossflow cylinder head and a similar main-bearing upgrade to the PA, producing 56 brake horsepower. Gone was the Wilson pre-selector gearbox. There were also 12-inch (30.5-cm) drum brakes shared with the PA and a new Bishop cam steering box. The body was now mounted on rubber-insulated subframes for greater refinement. At

LEONARD LORD

Viewed by some as almost a pantomime villain in the MG story, Lord made several important impacts on the marque.

Born in Coventry, United Kingdom, in 1896, in 1920 he joined Hotchkiss et Cie, which supplied power plants to Morris Motors Ltd. The customer soon took over the supplier; Lord became a production engineer at the newly renamed Morris Engines Ltd. and came into contact with Kimber at MG, to whom Morris supplied power plants.

The ultra-capable (brusque, shrewd, dynamic) Lord became Morris's protégé, thrown first into the Wolseley factory and then on to Morris Motors to shake things up and get each concern running efficiently.

This he did with aplomb. Lord instigated the formation of the new Nuffield Organization to bring all Nuffield/Morris Motors concerns under one banner. It subsumed MG, and Lord became its managing director. This effectively demoted Kimber. Having made his mark, Lord left in a huff in 1936 after Morris rebuffed his request for a share of the business.

Two years later he joined Austin Motor Company at Longbridge with one goal: domination over his erstwhile employer. Again, Lord excelled, becoming chairman and managing director by 1945. In 1952, after several attempts, he finally got his way, with William Morris (now Viscount Nuffield, after further elevation up the British societal ladder) agreeing to a merger with Austin Motors to form the British Motor Corporation.

He stepped down as chairman almost immediately, leaving Lord to, well, lord over his former charges from the very top. One of his first decisions was to reject the EX175 project; although to his credit, several years later he reversed that particular decision and it became the MGA sports car.

Knighted in 1954, Lord partially retired that year, became Baron Lambury of Northfield in 1962, and eventually severed his ties with BMC in 1966 before passing away the following year.

£305 for a two-seater and £335 for the four-seater, it sat equidistant between both predecessors' asking prices.

Trackside success continued unabated, with an unsupercharged version of the new Magnette powering Charlie Dobson to victory in that year's Tourist Trophy. If the J4 racing variant had seemed extreme, it had nothing on the new 113-brake horsepower Q-Type racing Midget; capable of 120 miles per hour (192 kilometers per hour), it was a truly formidable machine. Its 747cc power plant was the most powerful prewar engine, capable of producing 151 brake horsepower per liter at 7,500 rpm if equipped with an 8-inch Zoller supercharger. Abingdon's engineers appreciated that this was definitely too much for the chassis, as the Q-Type proved particularly hot to handle.

In April 1935 the R-Type arrived. A single-seater (as per the current Grand Prix racers), it represented the zenith of prewar MG design, with a state-of-the-art lightweight backbone chassis and fully independent suspension by torsion bars. It was still in the testing phase in July 1935 when MG suddenly withdrew from all racing.

The man who made that decision was Leonard Lord. Yes, the company's marketing and racing reputations were high, but there'd been fallout too. After an accident at the Mannin Beg event on the Isle of Man in 1934, officials charged driver Kaye Don with manslaughter (he served four months) in the death of his racing mechanic,

Frankie Taylor, during practice. Never a fan of racing, William Morris (by now, Baron Nuffield) found the incident particularly distasteful—although Lord had fired this particular bullet, there could be no doubt that Morris loaded the gun.

The overriding factor for Lord though, was profit. The sight of MG utilizing a plethora of expensive, specialized equipment (even the overhead-camshaft engines were expensive to manufacture, especially compared to those used elsewhere in the company) and pouring money into racing would have been anathema. More so, given it was on course to produce a record loss in 1935.

As well as his brutal decision with regards racing, he summarily closed the MG drawing office with all responsibility transferred to Cowley. The frenetic, pioneering period in which MG had risen to incredible heights both on the road and the racetracks of Europe was over, and for the newly emasculated Kimber it was time to toe the company line.

(Above) The Airline Coupe body style was built on P-Type and N-Type chassis and featured radical aerodynamic bodywork.

(Below) An MG R-Type (far left) and Q-Type (third from the left), pictured here at the Crystal Palace Race Meeting on the August 26, 1939; these models continued to break records and win races long after their cancellation.

1923

8/33 M-Type Midget

Models	Two-seater Roadster (£175), Sportsman's Coupe (£245), 12/12 (£245)	Max Torque	n/a
		Gearbox	3-speed manual
Construction	Steel ladder type chassis, fabric-covered body wooden bodyshell skeleton (Coupe, steel panelled)	Automatic	n/a
		Final Drive Ratio	4.89:1
		Steering	Adamant worm and wheel
Length	123 in (312.4 cm)	Front Suspension	Beam axle, on pivoted half-elliptic leaf springs, Hartford friction dampers
Width	50 in (127 cm)		
Height	n/a	Rear Suspension	Live (beam) axle on half-elliptic shackled leaf springs, Hartford friction dampers
Wheelbase	78 in (198.12 cm)		
Weight	Roadster 1,134 lb (514 kg); Coupe 1,302 lb (591 kg)		
		Tires	4 in × 27 in
Engine Size	847cc	Brakes	8-in (20.3 cm) drum brakes front and rear, cable operated
Engine Format	In-line 4-cylinder		
Carburetion	1 × 1.25 in horizontal SU	0 to 50 mph	25 sec
Max Bhp	20 bhp @ 4,000 rpm (later cars: 27 bhp @ 4,500 rpm)	Top Speed	60 mph (96 km/h)
		Fuel Economy	38 mpg (US, 31.6 mpg) (est)

1928–1931

18/80 MkI

Models	Two-seater (£480), Tourer (£485), Salonette (£545), Saloon (£555)	Max Torque	n/a
		Gearbox	3-speed manual
Construction	Steel channel section, steel-panelled wooden skeleton	Automatic	n/a
		Final Drive Ratio	4.25:1
Length	156 in (396.2 cm)	Steering	Marles steering
Width	60 in (152.4 cm)	Front Suspension	Beam axle, shackled half-elliptic leaf springs, Hartford shock absorbers
Height	n/a		
Wheelbase	114 in (289.6 cm)	Rear Suspension	Live (beam) axle on shackled half-elliptic leaf springs, Hartford shock absorbers
Weight	Two-seater 2,575.9 lb (1,168.4 kg); Saloon 2,883.9 lb (1,308.1 kg)		
Engine Size	2,468cc		
Engine Format	In-line 6-cylinder	Tires	4.50 × 19 in
Carburetion	2 × SU	Brakes	12-in (30.5 cm) drum brakes front and rear
Max Bhp	60 bhp @ 3,200 rpm		
		0 to 50 mph	30 sec
		Top Speed	80 mph (128.7 km/h)
		Fuel Economy	18 mpg (US, 14.99 mpg)

1932–1935

K1 Magnette (KA, KB, and KD engines)

Models	Saloon (£445), Tourer (£385)		Max Torque	n/a
Construction	Steel channel section, steel body panels on a wooden bodyshell skeleton		Gearbox	4-speed manual (KA & KD preselector), (Saloons ENV preselector)
Length	150 in (381 cm)		Automatic	n/a
Width	58 in (147 cm)		Final Drive Ratio	5.78:1
Height	n/a		Steering	Marles-Weller worm and peg with divided track rod
Wheelbase	108 in (274 cm)		Front Suspension	Beam axle, on pivoted half-elliptic leaf springs, Hartford friction dampers
Weight	Saloon 2,352 lb (1,067 kg); open 4-seat Tourer 2,184 lb (990.6 kg)		Rear Suspension	Live (beam) axle on half-elliptic leaf springs with pivots and bronze trunnions, Hartford friction dampers
Engine Size	1,086cc (KD Saloon 1,271cc)			
Engine Format	In-line 6-cylinder		Tires	4.75 × 19 in
Carburetion	KA & KB: 3 × SU OM carburetors; KD: 2 × SU HV2 carburetors		Brakes	13-in (33 cm) drum brakes front and rear
Max Bhp	KA: 39 bhp @ 5,500 rpm; KB: 41 bhp @ 5,500 rpm; KD: 48.5 bhp @ 5,500 rpm		0 to 50 mph	28 sec
			Top Speed	70 mph (112.7 km/h)
			Fuel Economy	38 mpg (US, 31.6 mpg) (est)

1934–1936

PA Midget

Models	Two-seater Roadster (£220), Four-seater Airline Coupe (£240)		Max Torque	n/a
			Gearbox	4-speed manual
Construction	Steel ladder-type, with steel body panels on a wooden bodyshell skeleton		Automatic	n/a
			Final Drive Ratio	5.125:1
Length	135 in (342.9 cm); Four-seater, 138 in (350.5 cm)		Steering	Marles-Weller, later Bishop cam
Width	52.5 in (133.4 cm)		Front Suspension	Beam axle, half-elliptic leaf springs with pivots and bronze trunnions, Hartford friction dampers
Height	51.5 in (130.8 cm)			
Wheelbase	87.65 in (222.6 cm)		Rear Suspension	Live (beam) axle on half-elliptic leaf springs with pivots and bronze trunnions, Luvax hydraulic dampers
Weight	1,567.5 lb (711 kg)			
Engine Size	847cc			
Engine Format	In-line 4-cylinder		Tires	4.00 × 19 in
Carburetion	2 × 1 in SU		Brakes	12-in (30.5 cm) drum brakes front and rear
Max Bhp	36 bhp @ 5,500 rpm		0 to 60 mph	23 secs
			Top Speed	72 mph (116 km/h)
			Fuel Economy	34 mpg (US, 28.3 mpg)

CHAPTER 3

A NEW OWNER

When Morris Motors Ltd purchased the company, the continued development of road-going and race models that had so characterized the early 1930s at Abingdon ceased. Morris closed the MG Design Office and abruptly cancelled the whole race program. With all decision making, and thus company emphasis, shifting to Cowley, it was time for the development, construction, and sale of a new breed of MG: from the SA and TA, to the VA, WA, and TB.

Although the TB had a smaller-capacity engine than its predecessor (1,250cc versus 1,292cc), the new XPAG unit was both more powerful and smoother.

Imagine the atmosphere at Abingdon after Lord's decrees (his own boss, Lord Nuffield, was no doubt fully briefed prior to the axe falling, as very little happened in his empire without his say-so). The hopes and ambitions of the MG's senior management lay in ruins, and morale must have plummeted. But there was little chance to ruminate for it was time to get back to Morris's original *raison d'être*: making road cars for profit.

The powers that be agreed that MG would continue building its P-Series Midget and K-Series Magnette, while the Morris Motor Company's Cowley headquarters worked on designing their successors. This could be construed as a minor victory, as the combative Lord's first instinct was to shut down production completely.

An upgraded PB Midget—and what was the last ever overhead-cam Midget—joined the P-Series Midget in June 1935 (the original instantly became known as the PA), with a larger 939cc, 43-brake horsepower engine. Intended to rival the Singer 9, it also had a close-ratio

four-speed gearbox, colored radiator slats (as per the 18/80 MkII), and a dashboard warning light that illuminated at 20 miles per hour and went out at 30 miles per hour to let the driver know they were in a built-up area.

At the same time the N-Type Magnette received a new grille and speedometer, while the doors were now front-rather than rear-hinged. Response to the two cars was good. The PB sold 526 examples (2,500 P-Types, in total), with 804 N-Type Magnette variants constructed. But both would have a limited lifespan and were in effect holding models until the new, more closely brand-aligned (to both Morris and Wolseley) pushrod generation arrived.

1935–1936: BRAVE NEW WORLD

When Cowley revealed the first new solution in October 1935, it was a case of back to the future for MG. Gone for good was the expensive-to-produce overhead-cam engine, and in its stead Cowley placed a good old Wolseley-derived pushrod unit.

The SA was a large 2.0-liter straight-six sedan that had more in common with the company's first-generation-proper beasts, such as the 18/80, than its overly sporting immediate predecessors.

As well as the engine change, a conventional chassis had replaced the now de rigueur MG unit, while Lockheed hydraulic brakes replaced cable brakes. With a wheelbase of 123 inches (312.4 cm) and a weight of 3,300 pounds (1,497 kg) it was the biggest and heaviest Abingdon car yet. As per luxury cars of the era, it was also fitted with a Smiths Jackall jacking system; this comprised a built-in independent jack at each wheel, operated via a hydraulic pump located under a hatch in the passenger footwell, with which the front, rear, or indeed the entire car could be raised off the ground.

(Below) The costly to produce but oh-so-sweet overhead camshaft engine, shown here in supercharged form, takes a last of the line, final outing.

(Opposite) Like the PB Midget, the six-cylinder N-Type Magnette continued in production for only a short time until the new, Cowley-designed cars were ready.

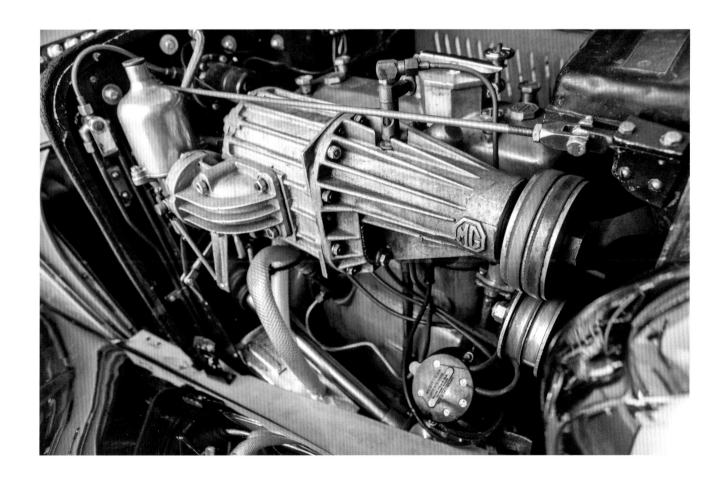

The elegant, sweeping styling was thanks to James Wignall of coachbuilder Mulliner, who designed it from the instruction of Kimber, as well as a finely finished cabin with leather upholstery and walnut fascia (⅝-inch [16 mm] plywood with walnut veneer), to take on those of the upcoming William Lyons–penned SS Jaguar. A Charlesworth Tourer and a very graceful Tickford Drophead Coupe by Salmons & Sons, with the chassis designed by Cowley, later joined the sedan.

It may have been significantly less sophisticated than what had come before, but priced at £375—compared to £399 (£445 for the pillarless four-door) for its predecessor—it looked like a very good value. Unlike the hitherto unproven SS, there was also the "MG" factor: a reputation hard earned over the last decade or so.

By the time the SA arrived in March 1936, its engine capacity had grown to 2,288cc and did so again to 2,322cc (good for 78.5 brake horsepower at 4,200 rpm) shortly after (although the 2-liter moniker stuck for many), and it had gained a close-ratio, part-synchromesh gearbox. The response was warm with *Motor Sport* stating in June, "A short run in the 2-litre left us very favorably impressed."

The 1,549cc VA quickly joined the lineup in April 1937, the SA's little brother in every way. It came in the same three body styles (although this time the Tourer body was made in-house by Morris bodies and not by Charlesworth) but for a lower price and sold well (2,407 in total).

Of more importance to the marque's traditional enthusiasts was the June 1936 release of the T-Type

Midget. Unlike with the SA, the Cowley design team very sensibly decided to keep the ladder-type chassis. The engine, though, was again of Wolseley lineage, which in aficionados' eyes meant a backward step to pushrod power. The reality was that with 50 brake horsepower at 5,000 rpm from the 1,292cc lump, it was still enough to give the heavier TA a small performance jump over the PB. In fact, it had considerably more torque and there wasn't the same need to work it so hard. The suspension, while still rock-solid by modern standards, was marginally softer. It was now an 80.4-miles-per-hour (129.3 km/h) car, but one that'd matured and was now as capable of touring comfortably (thanks to a high 4.87:1 top gear) as buzzing around country lanes or a racetrack. From a visual perspective it was pure Kimber—a modern evolution of Midgets past, but in a bigger (almost Magnette-sized) package.

There was a common denominator to the initial press reviews, as all believed it would be an instant success.

(Above) These brochure shots discuss the various benefits of the new Two-Litre models. As with the other Cowley-designed models, the main benefit to the manufacturer was cost savings!

(Opposite) MG continued to produce the P-Series Midget in upgraded 43 bhp, PB form.

SYDNEY ENEVER: THE ENGINEER

Born in Winchester, Hampshire, Syd Enever moved to Oxford at the age of fifteen. His school headmaster helped him gain a job at Morris Garages as an errand boy, but Enever's innate engineering abilities would see him excel.

After building his own three-wheeled car, he came to the attention of Kimber, who offered him the chance to join MG. He learned under the guidance of works manager Cecil Cousins and before long was heading up his own projects.

When MG's design department moved to Cowley in 1935, Enever stayed on at Abingdon in a liaison capacity. He'd play a key role in the development and construction of all of Abingdon's 1,100cc Class F and 1,500cc Class E record cars (both pre- and postwar), as well as in the company's war effort output.

He played another significant role in the postwar T-Series Midgets, but it is as the father of both the successful MGA and the ultra-successful MGB (developed after his promotion to chief engineer in 1954, a position he retained until 1971) that he is best known.

THE "GOLDIE" GARDNER MG

Despite the racing ban, MG was allowed to assist well-known record-breaker Major Alfred "Goldie" Gardner—himself the owner of a custom-colored WA Tickford, supplied by the MG factory for his honeymoon in the south of France—in his fresh attempt at the 1,100cc class. In 1937 MG purchased George Eyston's old K3 Magnette (known as both "The Magic Magnette" and "Humbug," thanks to the body styles it wore during its career [Eyston broke eleven Class G records with it]), rebuilt the chassis, and fitted it with a Centric-supercharged K-type engine.

Gardner broke Class G records on the Frankfurt–Darmstadt autobahn in 1937 before returning to Germany with a new Reid Railton–streamlined body in November the following year. This time with the supercharger running at 26 pounds boost and the engine outputting 194 brake horsepower at 7,000 rpm, it reached the speed of 186.6 miles per hour (300.3 km/h) to send more records tumbling.

A final outing at Dessau took place in May 1939 with Gardner recalling in an interview with *Light Car*, "On my very first run I knew that 200 mph was in the bag."

He smashed his own 1,100cc record, coaxing the EX135 to a scintillating speed of 203.5 mph (327 km/h). After an

In Dessau on May 31, 1939, Major "Goldie" Gardner set the record for the first 1,100cc car to break 200 mph.

incredible overnight rebore using portable equipment and overseen by Reg Jackson and Enever of MG, Mr. Kesterton of SU, and Mr. Shorrock of Centric, the EX135 broke the 1,500cc Class F at 204 mph (328.8 km/h).

"The Germans were most charming hosts," said Gardner. But just three months later, his host country set in motion a terrible cataclysm that enveloped the world for the next six years.

At a total length of 191 in (485.1 cm), the 2.6-liter WA was a bit of a behemoth. With 95.5 bhp available from its 2,561cc engine, it was also a considerable mover, taking just 14.5 seconds to go from 0–60 mph.

1937–1939: COUNTDOWN TO WAR

Cowley's new sales strategy was a success, as the fresh lineup sold in far greater numbers than the previous generation. Once the TA Midget's superior comfort and performance became clear, even diehard enthusiasts were won over. A smart but small-volume (just 260 built) Tickford drophead coupe joined the range. There were even two Airline coupes made. However, unlike the early 1930s when models lasted one to two years on the market, as with others in the Nuffield orbit, the new cars were designed to stay on sale for a considerably longer period.

This beautifully finished interior for a car that was competitively priced at £222 (£269.50 for the Tickford) did its sales prospects no harm at all.

With production and profits up, two new models were released: in 1938, the WA, with the first cars sold from December 9; and in 1939 the TB, which was an updated TA featuring the next generation 1,250cc XPAG (an inherently tuneable power plant, which powered MGs for the next fifteen years). The WA's 2,561cc six-cylinder engine produced a robust 96 brake horsepower, and that powered this 1,232-kg (2,716-pound) brute from 0 to 60 miles per hour in 14.5 seconds—exceedingly rapid for the period. Like the rest of the larger sedan range, its sporting capabilities were minimal; instead here was a consummate high-speed tourer.

The TA (here in three-position Drophead Coupe by Tickford form) continued the transition of the Midget from minimalistic sports car/sports racer to one with more of a touring capability.

CRACKERS, MUSKETEERS, AND HIGHLANDERS

"Jesus" Jones of the Cream Cracker Team wrangles his MG TA on the rustic 1938 MCC Edinburgh Trial.

Despite Lord's closing of Abingdon's Competitions Department, he couldn't entirely dampen its enthusiasm (and support, at first covert and later overt) for competitive motorsport. So, it was back to the arcane world of trialing, where it had all started.

That very British of motoring disciplines was still very much going strong and involved the ultimate tests of cars' reliability over long distances, up hill and down dale on the craziest of inclines (and declines, and hairpins, and . . .). Road surfaces varied from thick mud to gravel and small boulders. Vehicles that stopped were instantly disqualified, so competitors used all manner of innovative techniques to aid traction and thus continual forward momentum.

With the NE Magnettes prepared for the 1934 TT now redundant and no longer of any practical use, they were rebodied with P-Type Midget slab tanks and fenders. With a need for low down torque, an incredibly tight turning circle, and a low curb weight, each was modified accordingly (in came alloy panels, high-compression engines, underbody protection, and different springs and dampers).

A newly formed three-man team of privateers calling themselves "The Musketeers"—provided cars they named "Athos," "Aramis," and "Porthos"—triumphed, winning First Class medals in the 1935 Land's End and Edinburgh Trials, as well as the Welsh Rally (the victorious "Aramis" was Charlie Dodson's 1934 TT winner).

Meanwhile a rival team, the PB Midget–running "Cream Crackers," with their cars' distinctive cream bodies, fuel tanks, and front aprons with contrasting brown fenders, hood tops, scuttles, and wheels, was also picking up awards by the barrow load.

As this developed into a healthy rivalry, a third team, the Scottish-based "Highlanders," supplied with refurbished cars from the prior competition year, joined the fray. The rivalry between the first two was intense, with the after-event parties particularly ribald. Both tied at the 1935 Exeter Trial before swapping a long series of tit-for-tat wins, but it'd be The Musketeers who triumphed, winning the Motor Cycle Club's 1936 Championship.

Semi-official works support followed with each of the southern teams following their own path in terms of vehicles used. The Musketeers moved on to PA Midgets, then Magnette/Magna specials, and finally, in 1937, TAs (now painted red, departing from earlier colors similar to their rival's). The Cream Crackers, meanwhile, also moved from Midgets to TAs, but went down the 1,548cc (VA-style) engine route, and later a purpose-built 1,708cc unit—the latter was made available to police forces around the UK for fitment in the VA. The Musketeers opted for 1,292cc engines fitted with Laystall crankshafts and supercharged by a Marshall unit. Despite different approaches, competition remained close.

The Musketeers won the team prize at Donington in 1937, and the Cream Crackers a Motor Cycling Club Championship the following year. Success in the trials world was some consolation for MG, ensuring that it remained in the motorsport limelight.

Initially available with the same Sedan, Tickford, and Charlesworth bodies, the latter was discontinued from the range after only nine were made. During 1936 to 1939 the SVW models outsold the T-Type Midgets, showing just how well the buying public had received them.

Neither the TB nor the WA got into their sales stride (with 379 and 369 built, respectively) before all production ceased at Abingdon—although 17 WAs, 36 SAs, and 66 VAs would be built after September 3, 1939. Since its inception in the early 1920s, Kimber's creation had sold approximately 22,500 cars.

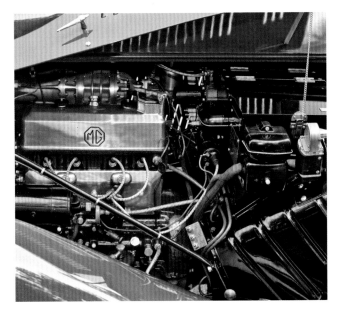

The new 1,250cc XPAG engine, as fitted to the MG TB-Series Midget

The 1½-liter VA was the third new MG to be introduced and was available in three body styles. This later 1939 example is a four-seater convertible Tourer.

1936–1939
SA

Models	Four-Seater Saloon (£375–£389), Charlesworth Open-Tourer (£375–£399), Tickford-bodied DHC (£415)	Gearbox	4-speed manual
		Automatic	n/a
		Final Drive Ratio	4.75:1
Construction	Steel box-section chassis frame, steel body panels on a wooden bodyshell skeleton	Steering	Bishop cam and lever
		Front Suspension	Beam axle, shackled half-elliptic leaf springs, Luvax hydraulic lever-arm dampers
Length	193 in (488 cm)		
Width	66.5 in (169 cm)	Rear Suspension	Live (beam) axle on shackled half-elliptic leaf springs, Luvax hydraulic lever-arm dampers
Height	60 in (152 cm)		
Wheelbase	123 in (312.4 cm)		
Weight	3,300 lb (1,497 kg)	Tires	5.50 × 18 in
Engine Size	2,288cc (later 2,322cc)	Brakes	Lockheed hydraulic 12 in (30.5 cm) drum brakes, front and rear
Engine Format	In-line 6-cylinder		
Carburetion	2 × SU	0 to 50 mph	25 sec
Max Bhp	75.3 bhp @ 4,300 rpm, 78.5 bhp @ 4,500 rpm	Top Speed	85 mph (137 km/h)
		Fuel Economy	19 mpg (US, 15.8 mpg)
Max Torque	n/a		

1936–1939
VA

Models	Saloon (£280), Tourer (£325), Drophead Coupe (£335)	Gearbox	4-speed manual
		Automatic	n/a
		Final Drive Ratio	5.22:1
Construction	Steel box-section chassis frame, steel body panels on a wooden bodyshell skeleton	Steering	Bishop cam and lever
		Front Suspension	Beam axle, shackled half-elliptic leaf springs, Luvax hydraulic lever-arm dampers
Length	157.5 in (400 cm)		
Width	61.5 in (156.2 cm)		
Height	61.75 in (156.8 cm)	Rear Suspension	Live (beam) axle on shackled half-elliptic leaf springs, Luvax hydraulic lever-arm dampers
Wheelbase	108 in (274 cm)		
Weight	2,380 lb (1,079.5 kg)		
Engine Size	1,548cc	Tires	5 × 19 in
Engine Format	In-line 4-cylinder	Brakes	Lockheed hydraulic 10 in (25.4 cm) drum brakes, front and rear
Carburetion	2 × SU		
Max Bhp	55 bhp @ 4,400 rpm	0 to 50 mph	15.8 sec (Tourer with screen down)
Max Torque	n/a	Top Speed	76.3 mph (122.7 km/h)
		Fuel Economy	25.5 mpg (US, 21.2 mpg)

1939

WA

Models	Saloon (£442), Drophead Coupe (£468), Charlesworth Tourer (£450)	**Gearbox**	4-speed manual
		Automatic	n/a
Construction	Steel box-section chassis frame, steel body panels on a wooden bodyshell skeleton	**Final Drive Ratio**	4.8:1
		Steering	Bishop cam and lever
Length	191 in (485.1 cm)	**Front Suspension**	Beam axle, shackled half-elliptic leaf springs, Luvax hydraulic lever-arm dampers
Width	60 in (152.4 cm)		
Height	68 in (172.7 cm)	**Rear Suspension**	Live (beam) axle on shackled half-elliptic leaf springs, Luvax hydraulic lever-arm dampers, Silentbloc bushes
Wheelbase	123 in (312.5 cm)		
Weight	2,716 lb (1,232 kg)		
Engine Size	2,561cc	**Tires**	5.5 × 18 in
Engine Format	In-line 6-cylinder	**Brakes**	Lockheed hydraulic 14 in (35.5 cm) drum brakes, front and rear, twin master cylinders
Carburetion	2 × SU		
Max Bhp	95.5 bhp @ 4,400 rpm	**0 to 50 mph**	10.4 sec
Max Torque	n/a	**Top Speed**	91 mph (146 km/h)
		Fuel Economy	24.4 mpg (US, 20.32 mpg)

1936–1939

TA

Models	Two-seater Sports (£222–£225), Tickford-bodied DHC (£269.50–£270), From '37 Airline Coupe (£295)	**Gearbox**	4-speed manual
		Automatic	n/a
		Final Drive Ratio	4.875:1
Construction	Ladder-type steel chassis frame, steel panelled body panels on a wooden bodyshell skeleton	**Steering**	Cam-gear
		Front Suspension	Beam axle, half-elliptic leaf springs, Luvax hydraulic lever-arm dampers
Length	139.75 in (355 cm)		
Width	56 in (142.2 cm)	**Rear Suspension**	Live (beam) axle on half-elliptic leaf springs, Luvax hydraulic lever-arm dampers
Height	53.5 in (135.9 cm)		
Wheelbase	94 in (238.8 cm)		
Weight	1,765 lb (800 kg)	**Tires**	4.50 × 19 in
Engine Size	1,292cc	**Brakes**	9 x 1.5 in drum brakes front and rear–hydraulically operated
Engine Format	In-line 4-cylinder		
Carburetion	2 × SU	**0 to 60 mph**	23.1 sec
Max Bhp	50 bhp @ 4,500 rpm	**Top Speed**	78 mph (126 km/h)
Max Torque	n/a	**Fuel Economy**	28 mpg (US, 23.3 mpg)

1936–1939

As above for TB, except

Models	Two-seater Sports (£225) Tickford-bodied DHC (£270)	**Max Torque**	64lb ft @ 2,600 rpm
		Final Drive Ratio	5.125:1
Height	53 in (134.6 cm)	**0 to 60 mph**	22.7 sec (est)
Engine Size	1,250cc	**Top Speed**	75 mph (121 km/h) (est)
Max Bhp	54 bhp @ 5,200 rpm	**Fuel Economy**	28 mpg (US, 23.3 mpg)

M G MIDGET

SERIES 'T.C.' TWO-SEATER

Underslung at the rear and upswept over the front axle, the chassis follows the successful line of previous models in the M.G. MIDGET series. Tubular cross-members and box section side members provide a rigidity capable of withstanding the stresses of competition work with a wide margin of strength in hand.

CHAPTER 4

POSTWAR MIDGETS

With World War II at an end and, with it, armament production, what now? Car manufacturing at Abingdon resumed with the TC, an all-important new product based on the TB. Yes, in essence, it still harked back to prewar days, but it was a roaring sales success. The later TD proved a pleasant combination of that earlier styling and improved mechanical specification. The last-of-the-line TF1250 and TF1500 kept the Midget fires burning, but the efforts of a privateer gentleman racer spurred the next generation.

Postwar production focused entirely on the TC, which was almost identical to the prewar TB.

The war years had been kind to Abingdon in that, unlike Cowley and its Coventry-based suppliers (the Morris Engines Branch and Morris Bodies Branch), it hadn't suffered significant bomb damage. Instead the workforce was able to focus continuously on a wide variety of wartime production tasks, including tank assembly, maintenance and repair, and the building of nose sections for the Armstrong–Whitworth Albemarle aircraft.

It had, however, suffered organizationally with the founder of the marque Kimber forced out in November 1941, after one too many disagreements with the Nuffield Organization vice chairman (and Kimber's then boss) Miles Thomas.

With the war over, large parts of the European mainland destroyed, and the British economy in a similarly perilous state, there was a severe need for home industries to export and generate hard currency. Shortages of materials abounded, with steel under strict control; the government released it for vehicles destined for export, but home-market production depended on manufacturers "earning" that steel from its overseas sales efforts. In fact, not only were all UK domestic purchases initially limited to "essential" users, they were also restricted by a sales covenant, with resale not allowed for a minimum period of two years.

MG had always focused primarily on its home market with export a secondary consideration, but a whole host of US servicemen stationed in Great Britain had sampled, fallen in love with, and even bought its prewar wares second hand. Many had returned home—indeed, some with their cars—with fond memories of blasting through Blighty's deserted wartime country lanes in an MG, and many more followed.

The cost of victory had been high for all parties, but, unlike Great Britain, the war efforts revitalized the US economy, and it stood on the brink of the greatest increase in GDP the world had ever seen. For automobile manufacturers that meant one thing: its appetite for cars would be voracious.

To meet the needs of a newly mechanized army that grew from some 40,000 vehicles to over 1.5 million, the UK motoring industry had been put on hold prior to and after the outbreak of war, with production refocused on the war effort. Industry giants, such as Lord Nuffield and the Rootes

The Abingdon-built Special had an aerodynamic prototype body sitting on a TD MkII chassis (note the very high seating position). Its aesthetics would provide the inspiration for the next-generation MGA.

brothers, were at the forefront; even smaller suppliers had to down their original tools and start anew on their appointed war produce.

That meant little if any time to concentrate on anything else. At MG, while the entire nation focused on survival and then victory, thoughts of future motorcar production simply weren't entertained. Once the war ended, from time and resource points of view there was no question of a new model being designed and put into production, so focus naturally turned to the prewar TB Midget. The SA/VA/WA types were to be dropped completely, as was the Tickford body style, with the new car to be built in two-seater roadster form only, for purposes of expediency, and in right-hand drive.

The TC Midget was identical in all but a number of minor changes. Engineers increased the cabin width—not an easy process, as it necessitated significant changes to the body framing and outer panels—and replaced the bronze trunnions used to locate the leaf-spring ends (which had constant greasing needs) with lower-maintenance, traditional rubber-bushed shackles; in addition, in came Luvax Girling shock absorbers and related chassis bracing. Despite these, the car retained the same hard riding, 54-brake horsepower, XPAG-powered, free-revving character of its predecessor.

The process of returning Abingdon to motorcar production was surprisingly quick, but incorporating necessary body changes delayed progress; as did a slow, limited supply of chassis; and the demobilization and return of workers. Despite the fact that the Luftwaffe had targeted it, the original Morris Bodies Branch TB body tooling had survived intact. Everything considered, the turnaround was impressive, and once the first TC rolled off the line on September 17, 1945 (the first postwar British sports car to do so), demand was insatiable.

1945–1949: DEMAND OUTSTRIPS SUPPLY

Autocar had, in June 1940, road tested one of the final prewar TB Midgets (CJB 59) to come off Abingdon's production line, saying, "It took the mind back over several years, flicking the dust off a certain chromium-plated radiator surmounted by an octagonal cap."

If the journalist had then somewhat wistfully allowed himself to turn his sights back to a less worrisome, freer time, then postwar buyers were to a certain extent doing the same. In Great Britain a blast in a new TC Midget allowed the driver to momentarily forget the privations and realities of postwar austerity; meanwhile over in the US, many ex-servicemen could relive the excitement (and perhaps freedoms) that their wartime exploits had entailed. Both could of course, revel in the extensive sporting pedigree that the badge naturally endowed on

The XPAG engine in all its glory—
its free-revving nature defined
the car's nature.

their new charge—there was no doubt about it, nostalgia sold. It took a number of years for the US market to reach its stride, but in Australia and South Africa, the model sold strongly from the start.

Those wishing to buy a TC at home required significantly deeper pockets than previously; in 1939 a TB Midget had cost £225, but in 1945 a combination of rampant inflation and a newly introduced purchase tax of a whopping 33 ½ percent saw it priced at a lofty £480.

The good news for MG was that its car had no real rivals in the marketplace. Many of its prewar competitors hadn't returned, and those that had, such as HRG (its 1,074cc and 1,496cc Roadsters cost a hideously expensive £812.14 and £967.15 respectively) and Singer, couldn't produce the necessary volumes to compete. With that the case, MG could in effect sell as many as it could reasonably produce.

Initially the TC could only be had with Black bodywork, although three interior colors (Vellum Beige, Shires Green, and Regency Red) were available. This changed by June

Demand for the new car was brisk, but with most earmarked for export, buying one for the home market was difficult.

1946, with Regency Red and Shires Green now optional exterior colors too. Sequoia Cream and Clipper Blue followed in 1948.

By this time 110 to 120 cars a month were being produced at Abingdon. Just 81 cars were produced in 1945, but 1,675 had been built by the end of 1946, with 638 going to export markets; although, not one of those had officially headed to North America.

The first road tests appeared in 1947, as did the new Y-Type "One and a Quarter Liter" sedan (more on that later), and almost all were unequivocal in welcoming back the Midget. Despite its higher price, in April *The Motor* said that, ". . . by present-day standards the car represents very good value." It acknowledged that the orthodox suspension with its solid riding nature could be found wanting on rougher roads, but still found in performance terms, ". . . the acceleration on the indirect speeds is such that most other cars can be left behind when the lights go green."

In October *Autocar* commended the fact that it remained traditional in appearance, having (by necessity) refrained from taking up a contemporary "all stream-lined" appearance. It continued, "The Midget is in no way more difficult to drive than the ordinary family [sedan], but given the type of driver who usually falls for such a machine—not necessarily a youngster—and who likes to use the gearbox, the performance becomes quite vivid."

By now 150 to 160 cars a month were leaving Abingdon and official exports to the US commenced, but by the year-end the number had risen only to 6. However, that year had also seen the founding of *Road & Track* magazine (others followed), and interest in small foreign sports cars was growing exponentially. Worldwide the Midget had steadily been gaining a very decent reputation—those that bought one knew exactly what they would get—and quite a following.

By 1947, 150 to 160 cars were being built each month. But it'd be the following year before US sales got into their full stride.

The TC Midget was perfectly at home in Hollywood, as this 1948 Eagle Lion Studios publicity shot demonstrates—spotty paintwork optional!

The year 1948, by comparison, saw 1,473 heading across the pond. So much so, Abingdon developed a special TC just for the North American market (starting from Chassis No. 7380). It had several special features—although, still no left-hand drive setup—that included a Lucas "Wind-tone" horn, twin tail lamps, flashing directional front and rear indicator bulbs, and bumpers front and rear.

By 1949 the postwar rush was over; US sales dipped to 522, and although the TC's RHD export market numbers hit an all-time high of 1,340, overall sales were down. The truth was that its once "vivid" performance was now struggling to compete, as was the traditional nature of its suspension, its semi-porous weather gear, and cold, heater-free cabin.

It was time for a new approach.

1949–1953: CHANGING TASTES

For prewar enthusiast, read masochist. In reality, that's what enduring a sports car's overtly stiffly sprung suspension had always entailed. The earlier arrival of the Y-Type sedan had left the TC looking decidedly unsophisticated, so serious changes were afoot.

Using a modified Y-Type chassis (the side rails swept over the rear axle, rather than under it)—complete with independent, coil-sprung front suspension; wishbones; and hydraulic lever arm dampers—was transformative in terms of ride comfort. Then came another novelty, the rack-and-pinion steering system devised by Alec Issigonis at Cowley in the late thirties, while in back the team added a hypoid bevel rear axle (as fitted to the YB sedan). In a sign of the growing importance of the US market, they now built the chassis in both right- and left-hand drive forms.

Working to a tight development budget meant that, mechanically, it was much as before with the TC engine continuing in service. However, the front brakes were upgraded to a more efficient twin-leading shoe design.

The wider chassis increased cabin space, while the body underwent a gentle evolution—still in every way a Midget, but with modern adornments, such as full-width front and rear bumpers with vertical overriders (a necessity for the US market). Combined with smaller, 15-inch (38 cm) disc wheels (the TD had no wire wheel option), its image initially took a hit in Great Britain, with some questioning its "sporting" credentials. How would the critics view it?

The answer was a resounding thumbs up. In January 1950 *Autocar* praised the fact that in appearance the TD hadn't gone "all futuristic," while lauding the "transformation effected in comfort" and "increased solidity" of the new model. It also felt that from a handling perspective the new suspension wasn't overly soft and had lost little of its lateral cornering capabilities. MG had re-jigged the TD's gearing to maintain acceleration, but at 160 pounds (73 kg) heavier, its 0-to-60 time took

(Above) Upright, elegant, and decidedly handsome, the Midget's size grew since the 1930s, but it remained a well-packaged and handsome car. MG always painted the TC radiator grilles to match upholstery.

(Left) US motoring journalists suggested that the lack of fenders left the model prone to the bumps and scrapes that North American motoring entailed. This example has makeshift rear protection.

GEORGE PHILLIPS AND HIS LE MANS MIDGETS

Ex-RAF man George Phillips was an ebullient, larger-than-life character, quick of wit and renowned for a faux-grumpy demeanor. In his post-service career he became chief photographer for *Autosport*. Reporting was one thing, but he was also a doer, and one with an absolute passion for racing.

He began competing (initially on mainland Britain only) in an MG TC bought from University Motors of London, fettling the engine for improved performance and soon after finishing second in class at the Brighton Speed Trials. Recognizing that the car's weight held it back, he then set about the bodywork, stripping it down to the chassis and commissioning Harry Lester to construct a lightweight body. Once complete, Phillips rebuilt the engine himself and modified it (sending the crankshaft and clutch assembly to Laystalls for balancing, constructing special valves, and using heavier springs) to give a higher power output.

The result was a unique-looking, low-slung racer that proved competitive in its highly lightened and more powerful form, first at the 1948 Manx Cup on the Isle of Man, where it finished first in class and fourth overall, and then (after broadening his competition horizons) at the 12 Hours of Paris race in Montlhéry, where it achieved a position of fourth in class.

Clearly emboldened by his success, Phillips then set his sights on Le Mans, securing an entry for the 1949 race. Panel beater Ted Goodwin built a fresh 20-gauge alloy

George Phillips drove his unique MG TC Special with Eric Winterbottom at the 1950 24 Hours of Le Mans, finishing in 18th place overall.

body, incorporating the necessary headlights and curved windshield.

The race ended in disappointment just after the 20-hour mark when electrical difficulties led to a rule misunderstanding and the team's disqualification. Never one to give up, the following year Phillips attacked Le Mans again, partnered with co-driver Eric Winterbottom. This time the TC Special performed impeccably, covering 1,760 miles at an average of 73 mph (118 km/h), powering to second place in the 1,500cc class and eighteenth overall.

a small hit, rising to 23.5 seconds—although *Motor* later tested it at 21.3 seconds.

The combination of a softer ride with precise steering proved a winner. There was no doubt that it was more comfortable, free of jarring shocks and with a marked improvement in road holding.

Another favorable factor was the asking price. At £569 (including purchase tax) it was just £41 more expensive than the outgoing TC. The British economy was having a particularly turbulent time, with the pound devalued against the US dollar in 1949. To Stateside MG aficionados in 1950, this meant happy, happy days, as the TD retailed for $1850, the bargain of a century compared to the TC's $2,395 price tag.

No wonder then, sales there went through the proverbial roof—helping to push total output (all markets, all models) from the relatively low numbers of the late forties to the heady heights of 7,451 in 1951 and 10,838 the following year.

From mid-1950 it was also possible to buy a slightly more tuned variant, the TD MkII (not to be confused with the TD2, an updated engine designation). Differentiated visually by chrome-plated radiator slats, a black-and-white MG radiator badge, and MkII badges on the hood sides and rear bumper, its engine output rose to 61 brake horsepower thanks to a higher 8.6:1 compression ratio, an improved cylinder head, and larger H4 1 ½ -inch (3.8 cm) SU carburetors.

Almost six percent of TDs were MkII variants, and it seems no two were the same. However, almost all had Andrex adjustable friction shock absorbers and the longer 4.875:1 final drive. They were significantly faster, with a top speed of 81.25 miles per hour (130.7 km/h) and a 16.5-second 0 to 60-miles-per-hour (97 km/h) time. The 1950 works racers were all MkIIs.

The TD retained the traditional looks of its predecessor, but under the skin lay the Y-Type's more sophisticated suspension setup and rack-and-pinion steering.

The "TD" Series M.G. MIDGET incorporates interesting NEW features

Overhead-valve engine developing 54 b.h.p. ● Twin S.U. carburetters ● Hypoid rear axle ● Direct-acting rack-and-pinion steering ● New facia, with separate speedometer and revolution counter ● Disc-type wheels with 5·50—15 tyres ● Lockheed hydraulic brakes; two leading shoes at front ● Coil spring independent front suspension ● Increased luggage space ● Piston-type shock absorbers ● Bumpers and over-riders ● Twin stop/tail-lights ● Twin wind-tone horns ● Glove box in facia.

Independent coil spring front wheel suspension brings a new smoothness to the ride and improves road-holding.

A 12½-gallon (57-litre) petrol tank gives a range of upwards of 350 miles (563 km.) without re-filling. Twin stop/tail-lights are now fitted.

In truth, owners of either variant could have any performance level they desired, thanks to the availability of MG's stage tuning kits. These offered a variety of power outputs, from Stage 1 (61 brake horsepower, as per the MkII) through to Stage 4a (about 69 brake horsepower) and beyond, to the use of Shorrock superchargers for truly hair-raising outputs.

It was a phenomenal result for a privateer team and one that impressed management at Abingdon, which agreed to build a prototype body on a TD MkII chassis for Phillips to use in the 1950 edition.

Given the moniker EX172, and unsanctioned by those at Cowley, it was developed in the depths of Abingdon using a beautiful aerodynamic alloy body by Enever. Road-registered UMG 400, the racer ultimately proved unsuccessful, dropping a valve after just two hours.

While that may be a hazard of the rigors of racing, Enever was dissatisfied (as Phillips himself had been) with the position of the driver's seat in the vehicle. Perched

atop the chassis frame, it diminished the body's aerodynamics, and his continued work on the concept—with the development of a new chassis—would lead directly to next generation MGA.

Technological advances impacted MG's racing outlook, as well. Mechanical updates to the revered EX135 (to keep Nuffield's noncompetition policies intact it was now known as the Gardner-MG, and loaned back to the Major) record car, first built in 1934, included the fitment of a supercharged XPAG. Good for 213 brake horsepower at 7,000 rpm, this engine powered the car, once again at "Goldie" Gardner's command, to six new International Class F records (in the 1½-liter category) at the Bonneville Salt Flats in Utah.

Motor Trend sent journalist Dick Van Osten down to Utah to cover Gardner's attempt, which he reported on in the November 1951 issue. His epic 1,444-mile road trip in a TD was part road test—". . . having owned a TC and an NA-type Magnette, I was interested in seeing how this model would compare. Believe me, there is no comparison!"—and part attack on the Class F Stock Car Record, open car division. Van Osten conducted the latter in a different, local dealer-provided TD MkII that ran without fault for 12 hours to set 28 new American speed records. After his return journey to California, again in the standard TD—also completed without issue—he concluded of its newfound comfort, ". . . the MG is not only an outstanding sports machine—it's a successful utility car."

Over on the track, things were also changing. Where the TC had proven uncompetitive—in 1949, three private cars prepared with factory help had been comprehensively beaten by 1½-liter HRGs in Britain's first ever production car race at Silverstone—the TD fared better. First up was an impressive 1–2–3 at the 1950 Tourist Trophy in Dunrod, with Dick Jacobs taking the checkered flag. A follow-up victory in that year's Daily Express Production car race at Silverstone was the model's competitive swansong. It was now at the limit of its development.

(Above) MG made a left-hand-drive variant available for the first time. As with the RHD car, both the tachometer and speedometer were now directly in front of the driver.

(Opposite top) Finally a North American export version. It remained right-hand-drive but now had front and rear fenders, as well as separate, flashing front (mounted on the cycle wings) and rear (mounted on the fuel tank) indicator bulbs.

(Opposite bottom) This well-appointed cabin has a one-piece bench seat, with the tachometer directly in front of the driver and speedometer on the passenger side; luggage room was reserved for the small area behind the seats.

The age of standard Midgets leaving the factory in supercharged form was over, but that didn't mean one couldn't be specified as such. MG offered a wide range of Special Tuning for XPAG-engined cars.

Two seismic changes occurred in 1952. The first was the long-awaited merger between the Nuffield Group and Austin Motors to form the British Motor Corporation. This brought the belligerent Lord—who'd so unceremoniously canned the company's racing activities in the thirties—back into MG's orbit, with significant short-term side effects. The second was the promotion of John Thornley to general manager. If Lord was, as many suspected, anti-MG in outlook, then Thornley, MG to his core, was its guardian.

The final TD left the factory on August 17, 1953. An incredible 29,664 had been built, and of that number, 23,488 of them had been exported to North America.

1953–1955: A FINAL HURRAH

The TF Midget variants never would have existed if it weren't for the recalcitrant Lord. His overriding decision to hit the brakes on the intended TD successor confirmed the suspicions of some at Abingdon that the marque sat firmly at the bottom of his priority list.

Rather than a brave new world, MG revisited the old one. The prewar Midget type bodywork—fashionable when new, charming immediately postwar, but by now anachronistic—was showing its age badly, but, given no other option, it continued as is.

Short on development money and even shorter on time, the team of Enever, Alec Hounslow, and Cousins, aided and abetted by skilled panel beater Billy Watkins, set to work handcrafting a new body. The result, completed just two weeks later, remained traditional yet more modern in appearance. Lower set, with a gently sloping radiator and a more acute fuel tank, it looked longer, wider, and more dynamic, while the partly recessed sealed-beam headlamps (a first for an MG) gave it a more up-to-date look head on. It was all of course smoke and mirrors, as the unchanged TD center section meant the cabin size remained identical.

Mechanical changes were also minimal. The 1250cc engine received an 8.0:1 compression ratio, larger SU

ARNOLT TD: A PRIVATE COMMISSION

Having spotted two special-bodied MG TDs on the Carrozzeria Bertone stand at the 1951 Turin Motor Show, Chicago-based British car distributor Stanley "Wacky" Arnolt II commissioned 100 examples of the soft top and another 100 of the handsome coupe.

These were for the American market only and distributed (alongside his standard MG, Morris, Rolls-Royce, Bentley, Daimler, and Aston Martin fare) from his East Erie Street dealership in the city.

MG-supplied chassis were sent to Bertone to be bodied, before being shipped to the States. The process of building them involved welding the steel body frames to the chassis, with the doors themselves hinged onto the frame. This resulted in a much stronger, stiffer chassis than on a traditional TD. Despite this, and thanks to the use of an alloy hood, trunk, and doors, the coupe came in at just 40 lb (18.1 kg) heavier and the Convertible 20 lb (9 kg) heavier.

The ticket price of $3,585 was quite a hike from the standard TD's $2,115. But there was no denying that both were "lookers" with their attractive Italian styling. Both interiors had additional occasional rear seating and were beautifully finished in the finest leather.

Advertised as "the family car with sports car styling and performance," further luxuries included a heater and radio, as

well as optional Rudge-type knock-off wheels. The convertible also featured a simplified "one-hand-top" design, rather than the standard, convoluted MG design.

If anything, the coupe—with its elegant demeanor—was the more visually appealing of the two, but both were mightily impressive in terms of fit and finish. Just 67 tin-top examples and 35 convertibles were sold (impressive for a special-bodied MG, but not quite the 200 commissioned) before the chassis supply from Abingdon dried up.

They were not, however, the last of Arnolt's creations, as he quickly turned his sights to commissioning the Arnolt Bristol.

(Above) *Well-resolved side profile of Stanley "Wacky" Arnolt II's handsome Coupe; Carrozzeria Bertone designed and constructed its body, as well as that of the open-top version.*

(Left) *The Arnolt Convertible was very well proportioned and retailed for $3,585. It looked much more substantial than its TD donor, but its curb weight was in fact only slightly heavier.*

carburetors, and a pair of pancake air cleaners (the latter a necessity due to space). The net result was a paltry 3 brake horsepower increase. At the same time, the 4.875:1 ratio rear axle returned. Inside, a pair of leather-trimmed bucket seats replaced the bench seat, and the design introduced octagonal-housed instruments.

Released in October 1953, both *Motor* and *Autocar* were tactful with their opinions, but notably no road tests were performed. In March the following year, *Road & Track* admitted its staffers still vied with each other for time behind the test car's wheel, stating, "To drive an MG is sheer pleasure" and voting it "America's best sports car buy," while at the same time admitting that it was a "retrogression."

Retailing for £35 less than the TD MkII it seemed reasonably good value, but there was a fresh problem: the Triumph TR2. Here was a rugged, well-constructed, genuine 100-miles-per-hour (105 miles per hour [169 km/h] in reality) machine at only a touch over £6 more. Accordingly, sales of the new MG were down significantly on those of the TD.

With the beautifully modern, in-house Austin-Healey 100 (in terms of top speed it did exactly as its name suggested) following quick on its heels, the T-Series body style received one final rejig in 1954 with the fitting of the 1,466cc XPEG derivative engine.

The Morris Engine Branch developed this hitherto unused unit. With the engine now producing 63 brake horsepower at 5,000 rpm and 76-pound-feet at 3,000 rpm, the performance boost for the new model (discernible by "TF1500" plaques on either side of the hood) was reasonable. Top speed hit 88 miles-per-hour (141.6 km/h), and it nipped 2.6 seconds off its predecessor's 0 to 60 miles-per-hour time.

Better still, Lord—in momentary show of solidarity—gave permission for MG to craft a replacement for the famed EX135 record car. Built from a spare EX175 chassis and fitted with a naturally aspirated 1,466cc XPEG engine, EX179 again made MG's name writ large at the salt plains

T. Flack's MG TD does its best to fight off Stirling Moss's Jaguar XK120 in the 1950 Tourist Trophy at Dundrod in Northern Ireland.

EX175: IF AT FIRST YOU DON'T SUCCEED

There's no doubt that the EX172 project nagged at Enever. The new body he'd designed did exactly as intended by providing improved aerodynamic performance with the bonus that its splendid lines were both modern and attractive. Yet the fundamental limitations of what lay beneath let it down.

Aided by apprentice Roy Brocklehurst, Enever returned to the concept and designed a brand new chassis frame. Its strong, boxed steel featured scuttle-bracing superstructures, with far wider chassis members than on the existing T-Series unit.

In an instant, the issue that had dogged George Phillips at Le Mans in 1950 was solved, allowing seats to be set far lower in the cabin. Enever added an updated, production-ready, pressed steel body in an almost identical style to that of the EX172, but this time constructed by the Morris Bodies Branch in Coventry.

Underneath sat MG TF1500 mechanicals, with the 63-brake-horsepower 1,466cc XPEG engine, gearbox, and hypoid bevel rear axle. The factory fitted bumpers, a windshield, hood, and sidescreens and trimmed the interior, then the prototype was road registered as HMO 6.

When Abingdon presented Lord with their great new hope at Cowley in autumn 1952, he flatly turned it down. Just three

It took a while but Len Lord finally approved the EX175 prototype as the T-Series Midgets' successor. The hood bulge was to clear the XPAG engine underneath.

days earlier, he'd given the Austin A90-engined Austin-Healey the go-ahead.

Enever and his team quietly shelved the project, but it was just too good to be consigned to the dustbin of history. As TD/TF sales struggled, the team justifiably revived the concept in June 1954.

of Utah. George Eyston and Ken Miles set seven new International Class F records (twenty-five American records) between them, the latter powering it to a top speed of 153.69 miles per hour (247.29 km/h).

American dealers could once again happily highlight a new model's record-breaking breeding. The tone in the UK, however, had been set at the 1954 London Motor Show, where two examples were displayed without their identifying hood plaques and with no apparent effort to publicize the model upgrade.

MG sold 1,951 TF1500s in 1954 and 1,449 in 1955, (with 1,826 and 661, respectively, going to the US). When Lord also permitted the reopening of a BMC works

competition department at Abingdon, fledgling rally driver Pat Moss piloted one to third place in the Ladies class in that year's RAC rally. But the reality was that time was drawing to a close for the T-Series. MG had always been a forward-looking marque, and forcibly being made to do the opposite didn't sit well. The TF1500 was a fine car, but one now out of time.

The postwar Midgets served their purpose, allowing the company to restart production, gain a truly worldwide reputation, and prove that nostalgia did indeed sell. However, the next few decades proved that modernity sold even better.

(Right) The TF dashboard has a padded top and centrally mounted instruments sitting in octagonal housings.

(Below) Despite the cessation of MG's autonomy of its "racing early thirties" as this artwork shows, the T-Series Midgets remained very popular as privateer racetrack, rally, and trial weapons.

Safety *fast!*

SERIES 'T.F'

(Left) Individual leather-trimmed bucket seats, rather than the earlier bench seats, were now de rigueur.

(Bottom left) The 1,466cc XPEG engine of a 1954 TF1500 was a derivative of the XPAG and produced 63 bhp at 5,000 rpm. It also powered the new EX179 record car.

(Bottom right) A final hurrah for the T-Series Midget, the TF 1500 had altogether more grown-up looks thanks to a sloping radiator grille and lower front end. This example sports wire wheels (as most did), rather than steel discs.

1945-1949
TC

Models	Two-seater Sports (£375–£412.50)		**Gearbox**	4-speed manual
Construction	Ladder-type steel chassis frame, steel-panelled body on a wooden body-shell skeleton		**Automatic**	n/a
			Final Drive Ratio	5.125:1
			Steering	Cam-gear
Length	139.75 in (355 cm)		**Front Suspension**	Beam axle, half-elliptic leaf springs, Luvax hydraulic lever-arm dampers
Width	56 in (142.2 cm)			
Height	53 in (134.6 cm)		**Rear Suspension**	Live (beam) axle on half-elliptic leaf springs, Luvax hydraulic lever-arm dampers
Wheelbase	94 in (238.8 cm)			
Weight	1,765 lb (800 kg)		**Tires**	4.50 × 19 in
Engine Size	1,250cc		**Brakes**	9 × 1.5 in drum brakes front and rear, hydraulically operated
Engine Format	In-line 4-cylinder			
Carburetion	2 × SU		**0 to 60 mph**	22.7 sec
Max Bhp	54 bhp @ 5,200 rpm		**Top Speed**	75 mph (121 km/h)
Max Torque	64 lb-ft @ 2,600 rpm		**Fuel Economy**	28 mpg (US, 23.3 mpg)

1949–1953 (TDII 1951–1953)
As above for TD, except

Models	Two-seater Sports (£445–530)		**Front Suspension**	Independent by coils springs, wishbones, and hydraulic lever-arm dampers
Length	145.3 in (368.3 cm)			
Width	59 in (149.9 cm)		**Tires**	5.50 × 15 in
Weight	1,930 lb (875 kg)		**0 to 60 mph**	23.5 sec
Steering	Rack and pinion		**Top Speed**	80 mph (129 km/h)
			Fuel Economy	25 mpg (US, 20.82 mpg)

1951–1953
As above for TD MkII, except

Models	Two-seater Sports (£585)		**0 to 60 mph**	16.5 sec
Max Bhp	60 bhp @ 5,500 rpm		**Top Speed**	81 mph (131 km/h)
Final Drive Ratio	4.875:1		**Fuel Economy**	25 mpg (US, 20.82 mpg)

1951–1953
As above for TF1250 and TF1500, except

Models	Two-seater Sports (£550)		**Final Drive Ratio**	4.875:1
Length	147 in (373.4 cm)		**Steering**	Rack and pinion
Width	58.3 in (148.1 cm)		**Front Suspension**	Independent by coils springs, wishbones, and hydraulic lever-arm dampers
Height	54.5 in (138.4 cm)			
Weight	1,930 lb (875 kg)		**Tires**	5.50 x 15 in
Engine Size	1,250cc or 1,466cc		**0 to 60 mph**	18.9 sec or 16.3 sec
Max Bhp	57 bhp @ 5,500 rpm or 63 bhp @ 5,000 rpm		**Top Speed**	80 mph (129 km/h) or 85 mph (137 km/h)
Max Torque	65 lb-ft @ 3,000 rpm or 76 lb-ft @ 3,000 rpm		**Fuel Economy**	(est) 27 mpg (US, 22.5 mpg) or 26 mpg (US 21.7 mpg) (est)

CHAPTER 5

Y-TYPE:

A CAR OF FIRSTS

If the hugely successful Midgets took time to truly arrive in the postwar world, then the Y-Type sedans were "modern" from the start. In order for them to be so, MG went back to the future by raiding the Morris parts bin. World War II had intervened in the original development of these vehicles, putting the all-steel bodied 1¼-liter MG on hold. In a new era, this popular little sedan charmed the buying public and spawned an open four-seater, as well as a number of coachbuilt varieties.

YB, featuring smaller 15-inch wheels, a front anti-roll bar, up-rated brakes, and a more sophisticated rear end, joined the fold in 1951.

Recognizing the need for a smaller car to complement the SA/VA/WA range, MG developed a prototype 1¼V-liter sedan and had it ready to go by 1939. The timing could not have been worse, and World War II relegated the vehicle to factory wartime transport.

The T-Type Midget in updated TC form got the Abingdon assembly lines up and running again after the war, quickly reaching a sales stride and bringing in much-needed revenue. But the Y-Type, called the YA after the arrival of the YB, wouldn't go on sale until nearly two years later, in 1947.

Post-conflict and with the economy in ruins, the country needed smaller, nimbler, more affordable vehicles. MG made the rational decision to discontinue the larger sedan range in favor of such a model.

To keep production costs low, it was in the main constructed from a mixture of Morris and Wolseley parts, and in essence an MG version of the four-door Series E Morris 8. As such, and in a first for an Abingdon product,

it had an all-steel body produced by the newly formed Nuffield Metal Products in Birmingham. The main body pressings were identical to the Morris. But the fenders, trunk, and hood panels, as well as the running boards, were unique to the MG and endowed the 1¼-liter with its "own" style—albeit one quite similar to the sweeping lines of its prewar relatives.

Its cheaper-to-produce pressed-steel disc wheels were another first, but the most important firsts without a doubt were the incorporation of a precise rack-and-pinion steering system and Issigonis's pioneering independent front suspension. The latter was of an ingenious, space-saving design that used coil springs, lower wishbones, and a lever-arm hydraulic damper with a link that doubled as an upper wishbone. In combination, the effects on both ride quality and steering feel were transformative (and were incorporated into the later TD Midget). The chassis meanwhile was a robust steel box-section frame with side-members that under-

swept the rear axle. Power came via a single-carburetor 46 brake horsepower version TC's 1250cc XPAG unit.

Despite the privations of the immediate postwar years, MG took their cue from their earliest days and aimed their new offering firmly at those who were slightly better off than standard Morris clientele. The vehicle's nicely finished interior, with its leather seats, polished wood, and octagonal instrument surrounds, enticed buyers, as did the reasonable price tag of £525. The new model was also endowed with the Smiths Jackall jacking system also seen on the earlier SA/VA/WA range.

With an eye firmly on the export market, MG also made this its first offering available in left-hand-drive form, although only 327 eventually sold.

1947-1950: AN EVOLUTIONARY EXPERIENCE

Sales of the Y-Type were healthy right from the word go, helped no doubt by an overwhelmingly positive recep-

tion. The little sedan looked fetching, and although it wasn't a scorching performer (0 to 60 miles per hour took 27 seconds and top speed was 70 miles per hour [113 km/h]) like the very last of the prewar sedans (the WA), its softly damped driving experience was unlike anything journalists or MG owners had experienced before.

In May 1947, *The Autocar* summarized its characteristics as, "... quiet and smooth, and extremely comfortable to ride in at the same time offering typical M.G. [sic] roadworthiness." It praised its "all-round" nature that allowed comfort for the family and pleasant high-speed cruising while retaining "a high degree of driving interest for the driver who likes motoring for its own sake as well as for transport purposes."

For those with preconceived notions of MGs (even the sedans) as simply teeth rattling, noisy, and rapid sporting beasts, the Y-Type was a pleasant surprise. And, for those enthusiasts/masochists who still yearned for that, there was the TC—although they couldn't get their fix with a family in tow.

JOHN THORNLEY: MG TO THE CORE

First and foremost a driving enthusiast, John Thornley was enjoying a successful career as an accountant in the City of London when he purchased an M-Type Midget. His underlying passion for the marque drove him, along with two fellow enthusiasts, to become a founding member of the MG Car Club. He was its first secretary.

This brought him into direct contact with the company, and in due course Kimber offered him a job in the Service Department. Here Thornley's first-class people-management skills came to the fore, and in 1934 he became the company's service manager.

He subsequently ran the company's "Cream Cracker" and "The Musketeers" trials teams with aplomb, before being called for service in the build-up to WWII. During the war years he rose to the rank of Lieutenant Colonel in the army, earning an Order of the British Empire award for services rendered.

After returning to Abingdon, he became general manager of MG in 1952, yet still found the time to pen the seminal *Maintaining the Breed*, a history of the company's racing cars. In the complex world of the British Motor Corporation,

Thornley gave up a successful accountancy career in the City of London to join the MG world, first as a founding father of the MG Car Club and later as the marque's general manager.

the company required a champion, and in Thornley it had the perfect man. He fought in its corner—even when all hope seemed lost—driving it forward, ensuring its future, and he continued to do so well into the late sixties.

That same month, *The Motor* called it "an extremely creditable car, a model which we would unhesitatingly order for personal use." It did highlight its somewhat conservative (in other words, prewar) looks, but went on to say, ". . . it offers good performance and the benefits of a modern design of chassis. It is a car which promises to prove justly popular, both in Britain and abroad, for many years to come."

Buoyed by the model's reception, MG introduced the YT four-seater open tourer in 1948, purely for export. The TC's 54-brake-horsepower, twin-carburetor version of the engine powered this vehicle. Complicated and costly machinery now constructed the all-steel body, so the main body was adapted from that of the sedan. Retooling for

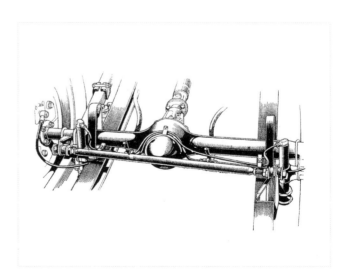

This *Motor* sketch shows the YA's spiral-bevel rear axle, complete with rubber-insulated transverse stabilizer rod.

The Smiths Jackall jacking system allows this Y-Type sedan to demonstrate its party trick, with all four wheels off the ground.

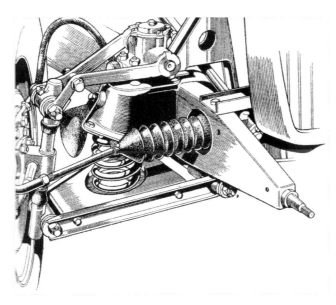

Another *Motor* sketch shows the beautifully packaged Alec Issigonis-designed independent front suspension and rack-and-pinion steering setup

the open-top variant's longer doors wasn't an option, so production of these reverted to the traditional method of creating a simple wood-framed skeleton and clothing it with steel panels. Those doors (only two, despite remaining a four-seater) were rear hinged, and it had a fold-flat windshield; a sporty double-hump scuttle; and a fabric-covered, TC-style dashboard. The fabric top could be stowed away, and for the US market it even had flashing indicators controlled from the steering wheel.

In open form though, the Y-Type looked a touch frumpy and out of time, certainly compared to the significantly sharper-lined Midget. It was neither fast enough nor fashionable enough for its target US market. Just 161 examples found their way there, with 251 in total sold. In autumn 1950, the company pulled it from sale.

A surprising—or given MG owners' proclivities, unsurprising—development was the use of the 1¼-liter sedan in competition. Despite a lack of outright grunt, its handling and road-holding capabilities proved fairly damned competitive.

Betty Haig and Barbara Marshall entered it into its first outing, the 1950 Monte Carlo Rally, and it performed well on a particularly exhausting and brutal run. Ultimately, though, they failed to be one of only five cars to complete it penalty free, and thus did not qualify for the final test.

1951–1953

An uprated YB variant joined the 1¼-liter sedan in 1951, although visually you'd have been hard pressed to spot the key visual differences: a reduction in wheel size from 16 inches (41 cm) to 15 inches (38 cm), the chrome bumpers now had overriders, and the incorporation of MG center medallions on the hubcaps.

Notable changes did in fact lie under the skin, where a front anti-roll bar and a more modern, hypoid rear axle (replacing the YA's spiral bevel unit) considerably improved the chassis. These made handling more predictable and eliminated the propensity for oversteer and excessive roll on enthusiastic (and over enthusiastic)

THE ZAGATO Y-TYPE

As with the Arnolt TD, another American businessman scented an opportunity to sell a bespoke-bodied MG. This time it was Roger Barlow, proprietor of Los Angeles–based International Motors, a supplier of imported vehicles (MG, Riley, Mercedes-Benz, and Jaguar, among others) to Hollywood-set notables, such as Clark Gable.

Having sampled and been impressed by a Y-Type sedan, Barlow believed that a modern body style, coupled with more power, a higher top gear ratio, and the standard car's impressive handling could create a customized, small-scale winner. He also hoped that by fitting a lightweight body—keeping weight below 1,550 lb (730 kg)—and adding an engine with a Shorrock supercharger, top speed would be in excess of 100 miles per hour (160.9 km/h).

He first visited Abingdon in 1948 to gain agreement for supply of modified running chassis, with steering columns lowered and lengthened, and TC exhaust manifolds.

Abingdon shipped one to Milan, Italy, where Carrozzeria Zagato set to work. The result was interesting to say the least. *Road & Track* in December 1949 was perhaps kind when it reported, ". . . the great Zagato has succeeded in creating a body having bold, yet smooth, appearance for the famous 1¼ litre MG chassis."

It's true Zagato had incorporated the distinctive MG radiator, but while the front end was pleasant, the curved door and

Only one Zagato Y-Type was ever built. Its unique lines worked reasonably well at the front, but the rear profile was Morris Minor-esque, and the side profile was . . . interesting.

quarter Plexiglas "Panoramica" windows (similar to those eventually seen on the 1963 Lancia Flavia Sport Zagato) were an acquired taste, and the rear end, positively Morris Minor-esque.

Alas, in the end Barlow's plan to produce 70 examples (in fact a combination of Zagato-, Castagna-, and Farina-bodied cars) came to nothing, with the whole idea scrapped with just the solitary prototype built.

approaches to cornering. The other main improvement was the introduction of up-rated brakes, with two leading shoe drum units now standard.

The YA continued to be sold alongside it, but for those who felt they'd benefit from the new additions, the YB could now be purchased for £635 (by now a £70 price premium).

In the 1951 R.A.C. Rally, Jim Readings finished first in class in a Y-Type, with Len Shaw in third place in the former Betty Haig car. Shaw subsequently finished sixth overall in a YB on the '53 running of the event, with the three factory-supported cars—the others driven by Reg and Geoff Holt—taking the team prize.

Better still was to follow on the racetrack. In 1952 Dick Jacobs, proprietor of North London-based MG specialist Mill Garage, blitzed a team of Jowett Javelins to take an under-1,500cc Class win in the inaugural B.R.D.C Production Touring-Car Race at Silverstone. That Jacobs also drove his standard YB (UHK 111) to and from the circuit made the achievement all the more impressive.

And then there were three: YA followed the TC, and they were soon joined by the open-topped YT Tourer. The latter's doors were constructed traditionally using a steel panel on ash frame method.

He repeated this feat with victory in 1953 and again in 1954, the latter with a heavily modified engine now producing almost double the standard output at 90 brake horsepower at 6,900 rpm. Bookending these accomplishments were his '51 Class win in a TD and '55 win in a ZA Magnette. Surely there was no better advertisement for MG than this. It's no coincidence that Jacobs sold more MGs in London and the Home Counties than any other dealer.

Despite modern underpinnings and its subsequent adoption by both the TD- and TF-Midgets, just like those similarly prewar-styled cars, the Y-Type's time drew to a close. Buyers wanted modern, sleek lines, and production (for sedans, at least) switched to the equally up-to-date monocoque method.

Still, overall, the Y-Type hadn't done too badly, with an impressive 7,143 examples of all three variants constructed, while its chassis, front suspension setup, and steering system (incredibly the latter two would still be in use during the 1990s, in the MG RV8) set the template for all "modern" MGs to come.

(Below) Car number 1, Dick Jacob's MG YB sedan, goes head-to-head with Car number 3, the Jowett Javelin of R. J. C. Marshall, at the 1952 Daily Express BRDC International Trophy.

(Bottom) Lashings of leather and wood lent each Y-Series a very urbane interior ambience. No wonder they proved popular with the buying public.

1947-1953

Y-Type 1¼ Liter (later known as YA)

Models	Four-seater, Four-Door Saloon (£525–£565)		Gearbox	4-speed manual
			Automatic	n/a
Construction	Ladder-type steel chassis frame, steel body		Final Drive Ratio	5.143:1
			Steering	Rack and pinion
Length	161 in (409 cm)		Front Suspension	Independent of lateral wishbone type, coil springs, Luvax-Girling hydraulic dampers
Width	58.3 in (148cm)			
Height	57 in (145 cm)			
Wheelbase	99 in (251.5 cm)		Rear Suspension	Live (beam) axle on half-elliptic leaf springs, Luvax-Girling hydraulic dampers, anti-sway bar
Weight	2,184 lb (990.6 kg)			
Engine Size	1,250cc			
Engine Format	In-line 4-cylinder		Tires	5.25 × 16 in
Carburetion	1 x SU		Brakes	Lockheed hydraulic 9 in (22.86 cm) drum brakes, front and rear
Max Bhp	46 bhp @ 4,800 rpm			
Max Torque	58.5 lb-ft @ 2,400 rpm		0 to 60 mph	27 sec
			Top Speed	70 mph (113 km/h)
			Fuel Economy	27 mpg (US, 22.5 mpg)

1949-1953

YT-Type—as above, except

Models	Four-seater, Two-Door Open Tourer (£525–£565)		Width	58.5 in (148.6 cm)
			Weight	2,100 lb (952.5 kg)
Construction	Ladder-type steel chassis frame, steel body panels on a wooden bodyshell skeleton		Carburetion	2 × SU
			Max Bhp	54 bhp @ 5,200 rpm
Length	164 in (416.6 cm)			

1951-1953

YB-Type—as Y-Type 1¼ Liter, except

Models	Four-seater, Four-Door Saloon (£635)
Front Suspension	Anti-roll bar
Tires	5.5 × 15 in

CHAPTER 6

POSTWAR MAGNETTES:

REVOLUTION, NOT EVOLUTION

1953 unleashed broad changes, as MG incorporated monocoque construction for the first time. Its new four-door sedan was born into the institutional instability of the Austin Company's merger with the Nuffield Organization and formation of the British Motor Company. To stir buyers' emotions, MG invoked the Magnette name of yesteryear for this car that was quite unlike its famous forebears.

The ZA dashboard top was steel painted to resemble wood, but ZB was all wood. Its speedometer dwelt in an attractive, semi-octagonal housing complemented by a dished steering wheel.

The continued updates of prewar output could only sate the buying public for so long. After the privations of the war years and its immediate aftermath, the fifties were the glamorous age of the jet engine and fashion, like life, progressed rapidly. The postwar Midgets, while still greatly loved, were by now adored great uncle in their dotage rather than the vivacious youngsters the original had been. Nuffield Group clearly needed to embrace change.

Luckily the management recognized that and tapped Palmer—flush from the success of his Jowett Javelin—to become its new head of MG, Riley, and Wolseley sedan design. The planned MG Magnette resurrected the most famous name from the company's racing past, but in an altogether different form, developed in parallel with the Wolseley 4/44. At the same time, Palmer also designed a secondary stream of larger, six-seater Riley and Wolseleys.

While all used standard Nuffield engines, gearboxes, and rear axles, there were two distinct body shells. Palmer

had free rein over styling, chassis, and suspension designs. The Nuffield board, passed over the larger Riley 1.5-liter (as it was too closely associated with the Riley marque) and Wolseley 1.5-liter engines in favor of MG's 1,250cc XPAG unit (designated XPAW when fitted to a Wolseley), which, despite its age, had greater potential.

In an MG first, Palmer designed a new unitary construction, which did away with the heavier separate chassis/body formula while significantly increasing passenger space. To add comfort to this rigid chassis, he added compliant, well-located suspension, independent at the front; a hypoid bevel beam rear axle mounted on semielliptic leaf springs with torque arm location; and, in another MG first, telescopic dampers all round.

Palmer's admiration for Italian style informed the new vehicle's aesthetic, discarding the now-kitschy Americana style (Lincoln Zephyr, in particular) that had so influenced the Javelin. A sleek, new, Italianate body was the result, with definite hints of both Lancia's

THE 1½ LITRE MAGNETTE

(Above) This dynamic 1½-Liter Magnette ad provides the perfect visual expression of the company's "Safety Fast" slogan.

(Opposite) MG advertised the ZA Magnette as a highly practical sporting sedan. Here it's photographed towing a 1954 Pipit caravan.

"Aerlux"-bodied Aprilia and B50 Coupe influenced by the Pininfarina-designed, Facel-Metallon constructed, Bentley MkVI "Cresta" exhibited at the 1948 Paris Motor Show.

Pressed Steel at Cowley constructed the body, with several subassemblies welded together on an assembly jig to create the strong, stiff structure with only the doors, trunk lid, hood, and front fenders nonintegral to it. The MG had a lower ride height than the Wolseley, so the sills and fenders were different. Up front it had a more modern, moderately curved version of the traditional MG radiator grille.

Aimed at the more eager driver, the car had a floor-mounted (rather than column-mounted) gear change, and the cabin instruments (including a speedometer set in a semi-Octagon housing) and switches appeared directly in the driver's eyeline ahead of the steering wheel. There was no rev counter. Leather seats, a walnut dashboard (with a metal top panel painted to resemble wood) and door cappings, and a standard heater and defogger completed a nicely turned out interior.

The full-width rear light provides the driver with an uninterrupted view through the driving mirror.

The hand brake is situated between the seats for ease of operation and is of the press-button release type.

Two chromium-plated fog-lamps are provided as standard equipment on the M.G. Magnette.

The fuel tank filler is concealed by a flush-fitting panel with press-button release.

The S.U. fuel pump is mounted in the luggage locker for quietness of operation and extra efficiency.

The radiator shell and bonnet lift up as one counterbalanced unit to provide excellent engine accessibility.

This period brochure shows a number of modern touches, such as the fuel filler, a centrally mounted parking brake, and the one-piece hood for first-rate engine accessibility.

Meanwhile behind the scenes, Austin Motors and the Nuffield Group finalized their protracted merger in March 1952. One of the newly formed British Motor Company's first orders was to delay the Magnette. BMC put forward only the Wolseley for general release.

Rather than out of spite, the company made this decision in order to incorporate the new, Austin-derived B-Series engine. The MG was the first, but by no means last, BMC product to have the new unit. Ironically the more pedestrian Wolseley sported the 1,250cc XPAW, MG-derived engine.

The Magnette experienced another setback that precipitated a significant change shortly before its October 1953 press debut at Nuffield House in London. On a prototype test drive on the A40 Witney Road near Oxford, an oncoming vehicle forced driver Joe Gomm to brake heavily at 75 miles per hour. The resultant violent axle tramp rendered the car uncontrollable. No one was hurt, but with the release date fast approaching, Palmer quickly ditched his innovative torque arm rear suspension arrangement in favor of the Wolseley's conventional U-bolt axle/spring setup.

1953–1956:
A VERY (UN)CIVIL WAR

The release of the ZA Magnette initiated a firestorm—mainly in the pages of *Motor Sport*—with MG enthusiasts typing themselves into a frenzy to write letters decrying the gall of the new upstart using the name most closely associated with the supercharged, six-cylinder K3 Magnette. How dare it have fully enclosed bodywork, an Austin engine, and, worst of all, an MG-engined Wolseley sibling!

What couldn't be denied was that, at £645 (plus £269 17s 6d purchase tax)—just £10 more than the outgoing YB and £61 more than the Wolseley 4/44—it represented surprisingly good value. Despite the indignation, the ZA quickly gained a reputation as a rugged, comfortable, and capable sedan.

GERALD PALMER

Born in Southern Rhodesia (modern-day Zimbabwe), Gerald Palmer exhibited a love of cars from an early age. At the age of fourteen, he stripped the Ford Model T family car that his father, Southern Rhodesia's chief railway engineer, had given to him, when he himself bought a replacement, and then constructed a bespoke boat tail body of his own design.

In 1927 he began an apprenticeship with Scammell Lorries Ltd in England, where he spent five years learning his trade. His first professional attempt at designing a car came when Chalenor Barson (a fellow graduate of the Institute of Automobile Engineers) asked him to design one for Australian rally and race car driver Joan Richmond. Anthony Fisher, founder of the Institute for International Affairs, funded the project, and the resulting Deroy was an attractive and mechanically sophisticated (with all independent suspension and a De Dion rear axle) two seater, if a little underpowered due to its 1.5-liter side-valve engine.

Still, arriving in it for an interview with Kimber in 1939 was enough to impress the MG man. Kimber helped facilitate a job as head of MG/Riley/Wolseley sedan design in the Morris Design Office.

Under the stultifying demands of war production, Palmer decamped to Jowett, where he was responsible for the innovative and highly regarded Jowett Javelin, a car *The Motor* called ". . . an exceptionally roomy, comfortable family sedan with sports car performance at instant command."

After returning to Cowley as chief designer of the Nuffield Group in 1949, he went on to play a key role in the development and construction of the new ZA Magnette, the TF, Riley Pathfinder, and the MGA Twin Cam engine, before departing for Vauxhall in 1955.

Available initially in just four colors (Twilight Grey, Metallic MG Green, Autumn Red, and Black) the car itself was very nicely styled, had first-class handling characteristics, and was capable of 80 miles per hour—as fast as its dedicated sports car TF stablemate. Its only downside was a lack of accelerative prowess due to its 2,467 pound (1,119 kg) heft, with 0 to 60 miles per hour taking a somewhat slothful 23 seconds.

Initial production delays, due to Abingdon adapting to the processes of constructing a monocoque car and early cars needing revised suspension, meant the press didn't receive a test car until the end of 1954. Based on the forthcoming praise, it was worth the wait. In its November issue, *The Autocar* said, "It is extremely comfortable, good looking and safe," and they called it, "one of the finer cars *The Autocar* has tested." Despite the late arrival of these plaudits it seemed the public already agreed, as just shy of 4,000 examples sold by year end.

The ZA endured several small changes during production. Opening front quarter lights arriving after the first

250 cars. MG replaced the metal top dash panel with wood after 6,500 had been produced and tweaked the color offerings in summer 1955. Island Green and Damask Red replaced metallic MG Green and Autumn Red, respectively, and three new colors—Steel Blue, Birch Grey and Royal Tan—were introduced. Sales of 8,925 that year proved a record for a MG sedan car.

Beginning in June 1956 with Chassis No. 18101, MG fitted the final 456 ZA Magnettes with the new, more powerful 68-brake-horsepower B-Series engine. Developed for the new MGA sports car, it had a higher (8.3:1) compression ratio, larger 1.5-inch (3.8 cm) carburetor, and a new exhaust manifold. To improve high-speed cruising, the rear axle ratio climbed to 4.55:1.

1956—1958: MORE POWER, AND COLOR

The new ZB arrived in October 1956, with the same engine essentially trialled in the last of the ZAs. The power hike reduced the 0 to 60-miles-per-hour time to 20.8 seconds and extended the top speed to 86 miles per hour (138 km/h).

Some changes to the new vehicle were mundane. While the interior received a fresh steering wheel and minor tweaks to the fascia, straight chrome strips replaced the ZA's "hockey stick" items on the exterior. But, just £718—£25 more than the standard ZB—got you the ZB Varitone, with very-of-its-time fashionable two-tone bodywork and a wraparound window. For £50, you could wow them with a "Manumatic" clutchless gear change system with the shift activated when the driver engaged the gear lever. With three pneumatic servos, two pneumatic solenoids, three electrical switches, one hydraulic and one pneumatic valve performing in unison for each gear change, it was as complex and unreliable, in terms of a smooth gear change, as it sounded. MG sold just 496 examples with that particular "upgrade."

(Above) You can identify the updated ZB Magnette by the straight chrome on its doors and front wings. A "Manumatic" clutchless gear change system was now available.

(Oppposite) A standard ZB Magnette featured the same flat rear window as its predecessor; trunk space was considerable, easily fitting luggage for four.

That same year, knowing the chassis could handle more power, Abingdon's Engineering Development Department produced an experimental Magnette Six (EX202) using a 2.6-liter straight-six C-Series engine. Alas, it came to nothing. Foreshadowing what was to come for MGC, it required considerable structural change. Incorporating Palmer's twin-cam cylinder-head design would have been more cost effective, but while one prototype was likely constructed at Abingdon, this idea too went no further.

In fact, the model was on borrowed time. Palmer had a quick dalliance with a one-off pillar-less coupe, but in 1958, despite the postwar Magnette's best-ever sales year (9,438 left Abingdon), the company removed the ZB from sale. The last ever four-seater MG sedan to be built at Abingdon was no more.

1959–1968: THE FARINA YEARS

If the initial furor over the ZA Magnette had been considerable, then the arrival of the ZB's replacement could have sent the very same people apoplectic. In truth though, by now the MG faithful were somewhat inured to the ways of BMC. The MGA had gone some way to restoring faith in Abingdon's modern sporting wares.

Despite still having the same basic B-Series engine, gearbox, and rear axle, the new MkIII was an entirely different proposition. Although it featured a new body shell, the front suspension layout and steering came from the 1947 Austin A40 with the basic monocoque based on the 1950s Austin A50 (and later A55). A cam and lever steering box replaced the rack-and-pinion steering. The only thing "MG" about it appeared to be its twin carburetor setup, while its stablemates, excepting the Riley, (and there were quite a few) had just one. Indeed it was the first MG assembled away from Abingdon, instead being built at the Nuffield factory in Cowley.

By now BMC was in full "badge-engineering" flow, releasing in late 1958 and early 1959 the Austin A55 Cambridge MkII, Morris Oxford Series V, Wolseley 15/60, Riley 4/68, and MkIII Magnette. Identical mechanically, structurally, and bodily, only individual grills, badges, lights, and interior trim differentiated them—oh, and in the MG's (and Riley's) case that extra carb!

The Magnette III's claimed "flawless sporting pedigree" belonged to MG output past, as the new car proved to be far from sporting.

THE "B-SERIES" ENGINE

Rationalization was the buzzword in the brave new BMC world. Management's overall targets were to keep development costs tight and ensure maximum financial return. As such, what was later known as "badge engineering" and component sharing were most definitely "in."

Three products of the Austin Design Office at Longbridge—the low-range A-Series, mid-range B-Series, and high-range C-Series engines—became central to the company's future.

Like the others, the B-Series was a sturdy and somewhat basic design. Its engineering could be described as ultra-conservative, but in the long term it endowed the unit with considerable benefits, including simplicity, ruggedness, and reliability, while also ensuring longevity. The relative ease of tuning and enlarging boded well for both future competition use and power output upgrades. It was also surprisingly indulgent of owners prone to withholding recommended maintenance.

Of a conventional cast-iron four-cylinder design, it had a three-bearing crankshaft with overhead valves operated by pushrods and rockers from a single camshaft. It housed induction ancillaries on one side and dealt with exhaust matters on the other.

Its lineage traced back to that of a prewar unit used in the Austin 10/4 and later further developed to 1,200cc

for use in the A40 Dorset, Devon, and Countryman. Now in 1,489cc (bored out to 3 in [73 mm]) twin-carburetor "MG" form, it provided the Magnette with a healthy 60 brake horsepower.

Its future held numerous capacity increases, exotic cylinder head addenda, and considerable competition success. But little could anyone have imagined its incredible (albeit, somewhat enforced) longevity—lasting as it did until the demise of the MGB in 1980.

B-Series engine output was now up to 68 bhp (from 60 bhp) thanks to a higher compression ratio, larger 1½-in carburetors, and a new exhaust manifold as per the MGA.

Unlike its badge-engineered sibling the Wolseley 44, the ZA Magnette's launch was delayed to incorporate the new rationalized BMC B-Series power plant.

While the ZA/ZB series Magnettes had dynamic lines, MkIII and MkIV buyers had to make do with somewhat more doughty looks.

Styling came via Pininfarina (hence the gang of five's "Farina" monikers), and wasn't entirely successful with its upright, somewhat bland front end, tire tracks that appeared too narrow, and finned rear fenders that looked as if they belonged to an entirely different car.

The MG's cabin was roomy, as was the trunk, and reasonably well appointed, with leather seats and walnut for the dashboard and door cappings. Dynamically it was a bit of a disaster, with vague steering, poor handling, and excessive roll oversteer at the limit.

Trying to rectify the dynamics, BMC released the MkIV in the autumn of 1961. Its lower ride height, wider front and rear track, longer wheelbase, and the addition of a front anti-roll bar, meant it was a different proposition to its older brother—if still not overtly sporting in manner. It was also the first MG offered with an automatic gearbox (the same unit would later be used on the MGB), another eye-twitcher for Octagon aficionados.

The MkIV soldiered on for another six years with little attention in terms of publicity or revision and largely forgotten by its BMC masters. Its reasonable sales numbers—7,812 MkIIIs in 1959 and 3,299 MkIVs in 1962—dwindled to just 688 in 1967. BMC pulled it the following year, just after the creation of British Leyland.

Nowadays, the ZA and ZB Magnettes provide a stylish and sporty fifties classic car experience. But the MkIII and MkIV Magnettes, while they do have their merits as a family classic, remain a reminder of an inglorious twentieth century end for a once famous name.

THE NEW GENERATION IN COMPETITION

Competing ran through the veins of those at MG, and thankfully the directors of the newly formed British Motor Corporation understood the publicity benefits that motorsport success could bring. As such, they formed a new Competition Department based at Abingdon, with Thornley as chairman of the committee and Marcus Chambers—who'd managed HRG's racing exploits before the war—in charge of its day-to-day operations.

The new Magnette's first competition outing was the 1955 Monte Carlo Rally, with three Maroon ZAs (KJB 908, KJB 909, and KJB 910) entered. To honor the victorious 1935 "works" trials, Magnettes MG ran them as The Three Musketeers: "Aramis," "Athos," and "Porthos." But there was no swashbuckling disposal of their competitors. The underpowered and heavily laden (two cars had three-man driving teams and all three bore weighty equipment) vehicles proved decidedly uncompetitive, finishing 178th, 202nd, and 237th. After a similar outcome on the RAC rally, the "French" trio disbanded.

With a view to B-Series power-output improvement, Palmer had by this point drawn up a twin-cam head design. Chambers wanted to build 500 lightened Magnettes endowed with this new engine for homologation. But the Comps Dept had yet to develop the organizational skills or clout to achieve such lofty ambitions, land-speed-record cars aside. Chambers used some lightweight alloy panels for the 1956 Tulip rally, but the car was promptly disqualified because the scrutineers

This photo captured Dick Jacobs in car number 32 at the 1955 Daily Express BRDC International Trophy on its way to a first-in-class (9th overall) finish.

The Grant/Davis Magnette ZA at a rally control on the 1956 Monte Carlo Rally

objected to the use of nonproduction panels. However, alongside using an MGA, Nancy Mitchell drove a Magnette to take the 1956 Ladies' European Rally Championship title. Its time as a rally car was coming to a close though, as sights now focused on the highly competitive Austin-Healey 100-6. Palmer's cylinder head design didn't see the light of day until 1958 in the MGA Twin Cam.

Surprisingly it was in fact on race circuits that the Magnette achieved a modicum of success, with Dick Jacobs, Alan Foster, and John Waller (the latter two privately entered) taking the first three places in class at the 1955 Daily Express Touring Car Race. Another win followed in the 1956 750 Motor Club's six-hour relay race, but the Magnette's greatest achievement was in Foster's hands in the inaugural 1958 British Saloon Car Championship, where he piloted a ZB to the Class B title, and fifth overall. This despite crashing and writing his car off at Silverstone and having to finish the season in one he purchased from privateer John Waller.

1953–1956
Magnette ZA

Models	Sedan (£645)		Gearbox	4-speed manual
Construction	Steel monocoque		Automatic	n/a
Length	169 in (429 cm)		Final Drive Ratio	4.875:1
Width	63 in (160 cm)		Steering	Rack and pinion
Height	58 in (147.3 cm)		Front Suspension	Independent with upper wishbone and lower arm, front and rear reaction arms, coil springs, and telescopic dampers
Wheelbase	102 in (259 cm)			
Weight	2,464 lb (1,117.7 kg)		Rear Suspension	Live axle on half-elliptic leaf springs, telescopic hydraulic rear dampers
Engine Size	1,489cc			
Engine Format	In-line 4-cylinder		Tires	5.50 × 15 in
Carburetion	2 × 1.25-in SU H2		Brakes	Lockheed hydraulic drum brakes, (Front 10 × 1.75 in [29.85 cm]) all around
Max Bhp	60 bhp @ 4,600 rpm			
Max Torque	78 lb-ft @ 3,000 rpm		0 to 60 mph	23.1 sec
			Top Speed	81 mph (130 km/h)
			Fuel Economy	est 28 mpg (US, 29.4 mpg)

1956–1958
As above for late ZA and 1956–1958 ZB Magnette, except

Models	Sedan (£693)		Final Drive Ratio	4.55:1
Carburetion	2 × 1.5-in SU H4		0 to 60 mph	20.8 sec
Max Bhp	68 bhp @ 5,200 rpm		Top Speed	86 mph (138 km/h)
			Fuel Economy	est 26 mpg (US, 21.65 mpg)

1959–1961
Magnette MkIII

Models	Sedan (£663)		Gearbox	4-speed manual
Construction	Steel monocoque		Automatic	Optional Borg Warner 35
Length	178 in (452 cm)		Final Drive Ratio	4.3:1
Width	63.4 in (161 cm)		Steering	Cam and lever
Height	59.5 in (151 cm)		Front Suspension	Independent with unequal length wishbones, coil springs, and lever-arm hydraulic dampers
Wheelbase	98 in (249.2 cm)			
Weight	2,513 lb (1,140 kg)			
Engine Size	1,489cc		Rear Suspension	Live axle on half-elliptic leaf springs, telescopic hydraulic rear dampers
Engine Format	In-line 4-cylinder			
Carburetion	2 × 1.5-in SU HS2		Tires	5.90 × 14 in
Max Bhp	68 bhp @ 4,600 rpm		Brakes	Hydraulic drum brakes, 9-in (22.9 cm) front and rear
Max Torque	78 lb-ft @ 3,000 rpm			
			0 to 60 mph	20.6 sec
			Top Speed	84 mph (135 km/h)
			Fuel Economy	est 28 mpg (US, 29.4 mpg)

1961–1968

As above for 1961–1968 Magnette MkIV, except

Models	Sedan (£737)		Front Suspension	Anti-roll bar
Wheelbase	100.4 in (255 cm)		Rear Suspension	Stabilizer bar
Engine Size	1,622cc		0 to 60 mph	19.5 sec
Max Bhp	72 bhp @ 5,200 rpm		Top Speed	86 mph (138 km/h)
			Fuel Economy	est 26 mpg (US, 21.65 mpg)

'Safety Fast' is not a slogan, but a principle as far as M.G. are concerned. We believe 'power in hand' is one of the great safety factors. M.G. braking (hydraulic fully compensated brakes with 9 in. (22·9 c.m.) diameter brake drums front and rear) is another. A third is the wider track and longer wheel base of the Magnette Mark IV with resultant increase in stability, road holding and general handling. A fourth is comfort. In addition to M.G. springing with independent front suspension, the Mark IV Magnette has the extra comfort of an anti-roll bar fitted to the front suspension, plus a stabiliser bar on the rear, along with new springs of lower rating. This M.G. thoroughness goes right through the car even down to the tyres, which being nylon corded, run cooler, resist impact and are stronger at high speeds. In total, the M.G. Magnette Mark IV is an exceptional car which combines the luxurious comfort of a polished wood fascia and deep leather upholstery with a superb 'Safety Fast' performance.

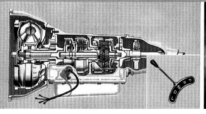

Solid built-in anchorage points for seat belts is an additional valuable feature of the 'Safety Fast' Magnette Mark IV.

A vitally important optional feature of the Magnette Mark IV is the provision of automatic transmission. Borg-Warner 35 automatic transmission — many millions are in use throughout the world — is unique in providing top gear flexibility with exceptional fuel economy at low speed — thanks to the low weight of the light alloys used. Indeed, this new motoring experience is a revelation — driving motions are reduced by as much as 70 per cent and you know what that means in freshness and lack of fatigue at the end of the run. This transmission will surprise the expert and delight the novice. It requires little maintenance and lasts indefinitely.

TRADITION THAT COUNTS

Volumes could be, and indeed have been written about the evolution of the M.G. It is a story unique in motoring history. It is a story of intensive specialization, of continuous striving after perfection. The International Class records which have been established by M.G. are too numerous to list here, but the most spectacular were those set up by Stirling Moss at Bonneville Salt Flats in August 1957, Class F Records for Britain. In a 1500 c.c. Special he achieved a top speed of 245 m.p.h. But it is not for prestige alone that M.G. engage in the costly business of making cars go faster than ever before. The real goal is . . . increased efficiency. How much will an engine give? How much can it take? Record-breaking cars produce vital facts — facts which have formed the background to the production of the new Magnette (Mark IV).

One glance at the beautiful walnut veneered fascia panel is sufficient to indicate the combination of good taste with the efficient clear reading of all the important dials.

Thanks to a wider track, longer wheelbase, and front antiroll bar, the MkIV handled better than its wayward immediate predecessor. It was also the first ever MG to offer an automatic gearbox.

CHAPTER 7

MGA:

A BEAUTIFUL PERFORMER

If the USA had fallen in love with MG via its prewar sporting cars, then the MGA cemented the country's postwar love affair with the marque. From drawing board to production, and on the racetrack, it excelled from the start and sold in the tens of thousands. However, it wasn't all smooth, as inherent design flaws adversely affected the ill-fated Twin Cam.

Clean lines remained unbroken by items such as exterior door handles. Opening the door via the interior pull cables with roof and sidescreens fitted involved negotiating the side curtain flap.

Despite its prewar design, the TF had done a fine job of holding the postwar sales fort, but by 1954—in a world of Jaguar's XK-range and the Austin-Healey 100—it was seriously out of date. Accordingly, total sales fell by 36 percent in just two years.

MG had of course been ready to move forward with the development of a new model as early as 1952, but in the complex post-Nuffield world of BMC, Lord instead gave the go ahead to the new Austin-Healey. All work on the experimental EX175 ceased. Faced with a fading product and the prospect of the famous marque becoming nothing more than a glorified assembly point in the greater BMC Empire, General Manager Thornley sought an entirely different future for MG. Persistent, tenacious, and focused, he used his powers of persuasion to gain Lord's blessing two years later to not only to restart development, but to reopen the marque's design department.

The project, designated EX182, proceeded using the same supremely strong experimental chassis that apprentice Roy Brocklehurst originally designed for EX175. Matters mechanical, though, had changed. BMC's radical rationalization program meant the existing T-Series underpinnings (XPAG engine and all) were out,

so chief engineer Enever instead instigated a redesign that incorporated the latest standardized B-Series units. These were already being used in the Palmer-designed ZA Magnette sedan, as well as the Austin A40 and Morris Oxford, among others.

The three-bearing 1,489cc four-cylinder engine's design, lacking the cutting-edge engineering developments to come later in the MGA's lifecycle, was a bit basic, but its inherent simplicity ensured first class reliability. To perk it up, MG increased the compression ratio with new pistons, a camshaft with a penchant for power delivery at high rpm, and two semi-downdraft 1½-SU carburetors—lifting output from a standard 50 brake horsepower to an altogether more satisfying 68 brake horsepower. Allied to this was a four-speed B-Series gearbox with synchromesh on all except first gear, a 4.3:1-ratio B-Series rear axle, and drum brakes all around. The latter two components were almost identical to the ZA Magnette's. The front suspension (modified) and rack and pinion steering carried over from the previous model, and it retained a number of traditional MG-type features, such as front and rear lever-arm dampers, twin six-volt batteries mounted on

Another Cutaway Drawing by "Autosport" Staff Artist Theo Page

Safety fast!

THE MG SERIES MGA

a cradle just in front of the rear axle, a "fold away" hood, and plastic sidescreens, in this instance with lifting flaps.

Without a doubt, however, the star of show was its new, aerodynamic body. It differed little from its Enever-styled EX175 origins—no bad thing, as the EX175 had been one hell of a looker. The new MGA's sultry lines, with elegant double swoop side elevation, finally brought the marque, kicking and screaming, into the new decade. At a stroke it made Triumph's TR2 look decidedly unwieldy, and it could now go toe to toe with the similarly sensual Austin-Healey.

A multi stage process made production of the new body and chassis more complex than with previous models. John Thompson Motor Pressing Ltd of Wolverhampton pressed the chassis frames, which Abingdon then welded and fitted with running gear and mechanical components. On the body front, Morris Bodies Branch in Coventry welded, trimmed, and painted the steel and light alloy pressings for the door skins, hood, and trunk lid before sending them by truck to Abingdon to be mated to the chassis.

Inside the cabin, elegant Jaeger instruments put to bed the fussy TF arrangement. The simple fascia included a speedometer, rev counter, and fuel, oil pressure, and water temperature gauges. With seats set between the box-section chassis side members, occupants sat much lower in the cabin than in earlier cars. Flashing direction indicators still came standard, and optional features included a radio, a heater, a demister, an adjustable telescopic steering column, a tonneau cover, a 4.55:1 ratio rear axle, whitewall tires, and center-lock wire wheels.

After its Lord-induced false start, MG was back in the game, and it looked to have a real contender on its hands. Of course, the proof of that came with its introduction.

1955–1957: REFLECTIVE GLORY

The delay in its release allowed the MGA road car to bask in the afterglow of the experimental Le Mans cars' fine performances while at its September 22, 1955, Frankfurt Motor Show debut. And it was only a bonus that it was

This launch car demonstrates the far superior aerodynamic lines of the new model, which was thanks to a significantly less upright demeanor. Despite a relatively modest power boost, performance was considerably better than the outgoing model.

so closely related both visually and mechanically (its 68 brake horsepower—very quickly upped to 72—was only a hop, skip, and a jump from 82.5 brake horsepower).

Commentators quite rightly focused on its appearance, which consigned to memory the upright traditional prewar lines. Gone were the running boards, cycle-type fenders, and vertical radiator grill, replaced with that new-fangled fashion of the fifties: curves.

If the TF appeared matronly, the MGA was altogether more Jayne Mansfield. "Its appearance excited universal admiration wherever I went, and the more discerning were quick to remark that it was beautifully made," wrote John Bolster in the October 1955 issue of *Autosport*. However, it certainly wasn't a case of all show and no go, as he continued with regards the new chassis: "The stability is exceptional, and the MG corners fast under perfect control." He also commended its competitive ticket price.

Sports Car Illustrated in its December preview also commented on the new model's aesthetics. "The characteristic family physiognomy has had a severe lifting . . . in this case a concession to progress and the laws of aerodynamics," while going on to purr, ". . . the new MG is an example of the coach works we've come to expect from across the sea." It seemed that buyers agreed, and in the few short months prior to year's end, MG built 1,003 examples.

In January 1956, it was *Motor Trend*'s turn to put it to the test. Like those before him, writer Walt Woron enthused about both the radical new style and its handling prowess, although he lamented the engine's puny (by US standards) 1.5-liter capacity. "I hope they will recognize that performance (and more particularly, acceleration) is what the majority of the American motoring public desires."

The remainder of the year proved Woron's supposition wrong. Far from simply wishing to burn off big-engined Chevy, Ford, and Plymouths at the lights, the very same American public (alongside those in all remaining markets) created a frenzy that had the new model leaving Abingdon at a rate of 300 per week.

EX182: THE LE MANS PROTOTYPES

Given the go-ahead to reopen the famous MG Competition Department, Thornley wasted no time in targeting the 1955 24 Hours of Le Mans race for his new MGA model.

To ensure maximum bang for his publicity buck, he intended to release the road-going MGA in unison, but the Morris Bodies Branch was unable to get the tooling ready in time. Changing direction, the cars were entered in the "Prototype" category, putting them up against highly developed specialist racing machinery—most notably from Porsche.

The four MGAs constructed—LBL 301, LBL 302, LBL 303, and a spare—deviated only slightly from the standard production car, so chasing an outright victory was now out of the question. Pitted against the racing Triumph TR2s with their bigger 2-liter engines and disc brakes, there were still kudos to be had.

They fitted their strong chassis—developed from the EX179 record car—with stiffened, yet standard, MGA suspension; a B-Series transmission, here fitted with close ratios; a high-ratio B-Series rear axle; and a B-Series engine. The latter had undergone significant testing at both Abingdon and Coventry, and the team fitted it with a special Harry Weslake-designed cast iron cylinder head. Its outputs of 82.5 brake horsepower at 6,500 rpm and 85-pound-feet at 4,500 rpm saw it somewhat underpowered compared to much of the field.

Its light, all-alloy body was identical to the later production car, save for the removal of bumpers and fitting of a high-output Lucas Flamethrower lamp integrated into the offside radiator grill; a racing windshield, 20-gallon fuel tank, Lockheed drum brakes, and center-lock wire wheels were the finishing touches.

Excitement filled the air on race day. At that time, safety precautions were minimal. Spectators packed the edges of the track, separated from the zooming cars by makeshift fences and bales of straw. Drivers made pitstops just along the lanes. No one was prepared for the horrific crash involving Pierre Levegh's Mercedes-Benz 300SLR and Lance Macklin's Austin-Healey that occurred on lap 35. Levegh's car catapulted into the crowd, breaking into three pieces. Levegh died on impact; the flying debris and engine-turned-fireball claimed more than 80 lives. The tragedy darkened the day but racing continued—although Mercedes-Benz subsequently withdrew. With a track

Delays meant that the "works" MG EX182 cars debuted before the actual production variants. Here, car number 41, driven by Ken Miles and Johnny Lockett, powers through a long, sweeping corner at Le Mans.

as large as the one at Le Mans, many were unaware of how bad the crash had been until hours later.

Dick Jacobs suffered career-ending injuries when he crashed his MGA several laps later, but the other two cars fought on, comprehensively putting the TR2s to the sword. Ken Miles and Johnny Lockett finished twelfth overall and fifth in class, lapping at 86.17 miles per hour. Ted Hand and Hans Waeffler came in seventeenth (sixth in class). Though the day's tragedies had a sobering effect on any subsequent celebration, the performance of MG's new model and hitherto unproven B-Series engine was a resounding success—although the company would pull its official race program in its aftermath.

The two remaining Le Mans cars, and the spare, raced again at the Tourist Trophy race in Dunrod, with less success. Two cars fitted with experimental Twin Cam engines, one of a Palmer/Morris design, the other of Appelby/Austin, gave a glimpse into the production car's far distant future. The former pulled out prerace and the latter retired, both due to considerable running difficulties.

Key to this was reasonable pricing of $2,195 in the States and £595 (plus £249 0s 10d purchase tax) in the UK. The latter—when you consider the £650 Triumph TR3 and £750 Austin-Healey 100—was particularly good value. Yes, the TR3 was faster and, from 1957 on, had front disc brakes (a first for a mass-production sports car), but the MGA was no slouch and arguably more delightful to the eye as much as the wallet.

Despite a similar curb weight and power output, the MGA's performance improvement over the TF was significant. It added 10 miles per hour to top speed and its 0 to 60 miles per hour came in at 15.6 seconds. It was in every way better—faster, with superior handling and more civilized interior and exterior accoutrements, including, for the first time, an opening trunk!

Taking a page from the Jaguar XK book, MG offered a fixed-head MGA coupe in 1956. Its pressed-steel roof and wraparound front and rear windows endowed it with an altogether more grownup look allied to more

(Above) The Coupe retailed for £699 (compared to £640 for the Roadster), better interior trimming, and wind-up windows, as well as exterior door handles.

(Below) The tin-top MGA Coupe looked even sharper than the Roadster. This example looks positively demure sporting the standard perforated disc wheels, rather than the optional wire wheels.

sensible fittings: wind-up glass windows and exterior door handles. The downside to this was an extra 100 pounds (45 kg) and thus a relative performance decrease. At £699 it was a touch more expensive than the Roadster, which had risen to £640 that May.

A detachable fiberglass hardtop available for the Roadster allowed MG to enter it in the GT category, where competition was a little less fierce. Come the end of the year, MG had built a total 13,410 MGAs. By comparison, only 10,838 TFs sold in its best year, 1952.

In 1957, the Roadster was now £663 and the Coupe £724. Sales figures outdid the previous year, with 20,571 cars finding homes. Thornley's persistence had been repaid—it was a strong opening 28 months.

On the competition front, it was clear by the end of 1957 that the MGA was heavy and somewhat underpowered compared to rivals. However, a special new high-performance variant was already on the way.

(Top) Both the windshield and the rear window are wraparound in profile (although semi, at the front), lending the Coupe an eye-pleasing aesthetic. The rear window features two vertical ribs for additional strength.

(Above) Engineers upgraded the B-Series engine from 68 bhp to 72 bhp very shortly after launch. MG's standardized engine specifications included twin 1½-in SU carburetors, as well as a different camshaft profile and manifold.

1958–1960:
HIGH EXPECTATIONS

If the standard MGA had racing kudos, then the new Twin Cam, with its engine derived directly from Stirling Moss's EX181 record-breaker and the un-supercharged EX179 before it, was positively bathed in reflective glory from the very start.

Palmer first conceived of a Twin Cam cylinder head as far back as 1954. Originally envisaged as a high-performance conversion for sports cars, the design concept went to the Morris Engines Branch in Coventry for further development. However, Lord also commissioned a design from the Austin engine design team at Longbridge, creating a mini engine arms race. Being restricted to using the existing engine block handicapped Palmer—the company allowed the Austin team to create a new design. The competition ended after the 1955 Dunrod Tourist Trophy race. Satisfyingly for Palmer and his team, the Austin unit was no more powerful than the standard pushrod engine it was vying to replace, and it was junked.

With the road now open for the Palmer design, the new Twin Cam model used a standard B-Series cylinder block bored out from 2.875 inches (73.025 mm) to 3 inches (75.4 mm). In came heavily domed pistons, a new connecting rod design, and an ultra-high 9.9:1 compression ratio.

The light alloy cylinder head, fed by twin semidown-draft 1¾-inch (4.4 cm) SU carburetors, had Jaguar/Coventry Climax-style valve operation by inverted bucket-type tappets. On paper the initial results looked impressive, with the new unit offering a heady 108 brake horsepower at 6,700 rpm. It seemed MG had another road-going winner on its hands and with it a fresh basis for attacking the 1,600cc competition classes.

Chassis changes were minimal, and both gearbox and gearing remained the same. Similarly the suspension was relatively untouched, save for raised front spring rates. But the biggest additions came at the wheels, which adopted four-wheel Dunlop disc brakes and Dunlop disc wheels (there was no wire wheel option for the Twin

This period US MGA ad played heavily on the model's racing prowess, and why not?

The Palmer-designed, Morris Engines–built, Twin Cam engine has an 80° line between valves. Although heavier than the pushrod overhead valve unit, the new car retained the same exemplary levels of road holding.

EX181: THE ROARING RAINDROP

MG's land-speed record cars played a critical part in the development of the MGA, and continued to influence the model's Twin Cam evolution. In 1956 EX179 used an un-supercharged version of the experimental Twin Cam engine to break the flying 10-mile (16-km) record, as well as a number of other endurance records.

Constructed to replace the famous EX135, which with Lt. Col. A.T. "Goldie" Garner at the wheel had set an incredible 34 international records between 1938 and 1952, the new EX181 descended upon the Bonneville Salt Flats in 1957 for an attack on the 1.1–1.5-liter Class F category.

It featured a 290-brake-horsepower, 516 lb-ft, Shorrock supercharged, twin-camshaft 1,489cc B-Series engine driving the rear wheels. This was housed amidships in an MG ladder-type chassis with a narrow 3' 6" (107 cm) front track that tapered at the rear, passing between the wheels, reducing the track to 2' 6 ¾" (78 cm).

MGA-derived suspension; a De Dion rear axle; rear inboard Girling disc brakes to save weight—there were no front brakes; rack-and-pinion steering; a four-speed manual gearbox; and Dunlop 24" (61 cm) OD tires completed a package clothed in an otherworldly light alloy 18-gauge Hiduminium 33

aerodynamic body. Its supremely efficient aerofoil form had been wind tunnel tested, and the entire car weighed just 1,642 lb (744.8 kg).

On Friday, August 23, racing driver Stirling Moss climbed into the tiny nose-housed driver's compartment, started up the engine—running on an 86% methanol, nitrobenzene, and sulfuric ether mix—and proceeded to blitz the previous record of 203 mph. The car achieved 245.64 mph for the flying kilometer, 245.11 mph for the mile, and broke five world records and another five US records.

Two years later on October 3, 1959, Phil Hill took to the salt flats in EX181—this time with an overbored 1,506cc, 300-brake-horsepower version of the same engine—and set yet more records: 254.91 and 254.53 mph respectively, this time in the Class E up-to-2,000cc category.

Promptly retired, the world's fastest "Fifteen Hundred" and "Two Thousand" remained MG's final, and quickest, land speed record car.

(Above) *On Friday, August 23, 1957, at the Bonneville Salt Flats, Utah, EX181—"The Roaring Raindrop"—accelerated to a towering top speed of 245.64 mph.*

(Left) *Stirling Moss is in preparatory mode in the EX181 cabin prior to his successful attack on the international land speed class F (1,100cc–1,500cc).*

Cam). The steering gear was also approximately 1 inch (2.5 cm) further forward to clear the substantially bulkier engine, with longer and stronger steering arms used.

Though there were few visual changes, the wheels gave the game away even at a distance. Up close, additional "Twin Cam" badges on the trunk lid and along the scuttle vents were noticeable. This lack of differentiation for MG's high-performance model became a recurring theme over the next two decades.

Standard issue in the cabin were a Rexine-covered dashboard, a new speedometer, and a rev counter. Options included an oil cooler, a close-ratio gearbox, padded competition seats, and the 4.55:1 rear axle.

Introduced to the press at the military test track in Chobham, Surrey, on July 15, 1958, the stage was set for the new model to excel.

Early opinions on the Twin Cam were mainly positive. "Power builds up noticeably after the engine tops 3,500 rpm; by the time 4,000 rpm is reached it really takes hold and the little car shows its potential performance," said *Autocar* in July 1958. It similarly praised the car's high-speed legs, which allowed it to cruise happily at 100 miles per hour on Continental roads. However, there were early signs of potential issues: "It also used a considerable amount of oil; five pints were added to the sump during one journey of 800 miles, and an overall oil-consumption figure of 1020 mpg was recorded."

There was no doubt the Twin Cam revved harder and was an altogether different performance proposition, but performance-testing results varied greatly and seemed highly dependent on conditions. *Autocar*'s 0 to 60-miles-per-hour time of 13.3 seconds was particularly disappointing for a car that, although heavier (a fraction over 100 pounds (45 kg) more than its pushrod equivalent), had, on paper at least, significantly more oomph. In North America, *Sport Car Illustrated* seconded this

The ultimate version of the MGA lasted only a short time in production before disappearing; the pushrod 1600 and 1600 MkII held the sales fort.

in October: "The results, while good were not terribly impressive," and in testing, the same—admittedly hard worked—press car in July 1958 experienced an engine in meltdown, "Power was very obviously down, oil consumption was up, water temperature stayed high, it pinged piteously at any but the lowest ignition setting and it 'ran on' like a berserk diesel."

The magazine's summation of that car's power unit as "... a very unhappy, unhealthy engine" was, in a microcosm, what private Twin Cam owners were experiencing. Instead of a brave new performance world, MG found itself facing one of engine failures and warranty claims. The high compression ratio made timing settings critical, as was the use of high-quality, five-star fuel. Deviate from this, and peril would soon be upon you via the medium of holed pistons. Perhaps, in retrospect, record car testing development using an 86-percent methanol mixture wasn't indicative of real-world conditions. There were also issues with the cooling system and with tappet buckets jamming.

As if that weren't enough, at £843 (£904 for the coupe) it was significantly pricier than the £699 Triumph TR3 and fellow (more corporately favored) BMC product, the £817 Austin-Healey 100/6—never mind that both were faster and free of mechanical histrionics. It took four piston type changes dropping the compression ratio to 8.3:1 before Abingdon's engineers began getting a handle on the issues.

In the meantime, pushrod MGA sales were off the chart: 20,571 in 1957 and 16,122 the following year. Spurred on by these numbers, and by specifications of competitors' cars, MG released the new 1600 in May 1959. The slightly modified body style included amber indicator lenses and separate flashing indicators and lamps at the rear. The Twin Cam used this new body, from chassis number 2192 onward.

Standardized with the Twin Cam, the engine block was now 1,588cc and housed stronger internals, including the big end bearings. With 79.5 brake horsepower on tap, it meant the new car was a bona fide

(Above) Chic steel wheels, shod in 5.90-section Dunlop RS4 Roadspeed tires, hide the Twin Cam model's up-rated all-wheel disc brakes.

(Opposite top) The extra performance from the Twin Cam engine was considerable, but running issues quickly became apparent. MG engineers had largely fixed these, then the model was discontinued.

(Opposite bottom) The Twin Cam scuttle vent and trunk lid badges, as well as the model-specific center-lock Dunlop steel wheels, were all that differentiated the new model from the standard car.

100-miles-per-hour steed. It also now had the stopping power to match, thanks to Lockheed 11-inch (279 mm) front disc brakes (drums remained standard fitment at the rear).

The new model was an immediate success. By May, 7,644 1500s had left Abingdon, and come the end of the year a further 14,156 1600s had joined them. By comparison, the specialist Twin Cam, which had shifted 541 in its first year, sold just 1,519.

The Twin Cam did fare better in competition, with two coupes taking second and third in class at the 12 Hours of Sebring race in Florida. But the continued excellence of the Austin-Healey 100-6, also prepared and run by the BMC Competition Department at Abingdon, curtailed the Twin Cam's hopes of a successful rallying career.

Still, the Twin Cam run by Ted Lund as a privateer entry at Le Mans in 1960 saw some success. This car with its UK registration, SRX210, was in effect a "works" prepared car submitted under the North Western Centre of the MG Car Club banner. It had raced there in 1959 using an original 1955 prototype body but was forced to pull out after hitting an Alsatian dog. For 1960, chief engineer Don Hayter used coupe doors, roof, and wrap-around windshield to convert its light alloy body, and enlarged its engine to 1,762cc. Along with Colin Escott, Lund piloted the car to a first in class finish (2-liter class) and a highly impressive thirteenth overall.

Back on the road though, the end was nigh. As the 1600 went from strength to strength and sold 16,930, the factory made just 51 Twin Cams in 1960. As Abingdon

Here's EX181 back on a record charge, this time with Phil Hill behind the wheel. At 254.53 mph, they saw yet more records tumble on the Utah Salt Flats.

PECO: MORE GO, LESS WOE

With its race- and record car-developed engine, the new Twin Cam was an exciting and intoxicating proposition, but it wasn't the only game in town. The Performance Equipment Company of Liverpool also offered a performance boost, via its supercharging kit for the standard MGA.

The kit comprised a new bolt-on exhaust and intake systems, as well as a low-pressure Roots-style supercharger. Developed by a team of consultant engineers working under managing director Vernon H. Farthing, the exhaust system featured a straight through silencer with a special, built-in "pulse rectifier" resonating chamber to negate reverse exhaust shock waves. Farthing was a fast-driving enthusiast and a specialist in gas flow. His concerns supplied, among others, the Atomic Energy Research Establishment.

The only other requirements were a Peco-cast manifold, a special carburetor needle, and a competition clutch. A reasonably knowledgeable enthusiast could fit the entire shebang. Visually, the only identifiers were the twin-exit exhaust silencer and tiny Peco transfers on the trunk, fenders, and hood.

Autocar was rightly impressed, writing in its June 1958 issue, ". . . the power under the sole of one's shoe was right out of the ordinary reckoning for a car of this size."

With a 0–60 mph time of 13.1 sec, it beat the Twin Cam by 0.2 sec. Best of all, from the buyer's perspective, it only cost roughly a third of that model's price increase. Not only was it faster and cheaper, in hindsight it was a lot less hassle.

The Performance Equipment Company of Liverpool offered full supercharging kits and tuning options ranging from exhaust-boosting tailpipe designs to bespoke manifolding.

pulled the plug on its exotic MGA, the irony was that, as Lund had demonstrated on track, its engine woes had by now been rectified and it was now more than capable of being the scintillating range-topping model it was always intended to be.

1961–1962:
A FINAL FLOURISH

The demise of the Twin Cam saddled MG with a surfeit of its special components. To use up this supply, it launched a "De Luxe" model that combined the 1600 pushrod engine with surplus items. Although it never appeared in a sales brochure, it could be had in both Roadster and Tourer forms. There appeared to be no definitive combination, as buyers could specify all or some of the additions. And, just to confuse matters, the South African badged "De Luxe" had no Twin Cam components at all. Initially built on a Twin Cam chassis, these soon gave way to standard units.

A new 1600 MkII arrived in June 1961, with light body styling changes—including Mini-sourced rear light clusters mounted on a reworked rear panel, a rejigged front grill, 1600 MkII badges . . . and a new, 1,622cc engine. Comprehensively improved, with a stronger bottom end and improved cylinder head, its fatter torque curve allowed fitment of a higher-ratio rear axle and made it an altogether sweeter motorway (and freeway) proposition. And with 90 brake horsepower, it was almost as fast as the outgoing Twin Cam. It too could be ordered in "De Luxe" form.

In September 1961 *Road and Track* was in no doubt that the MGA remained *the* sports car to beat: ". . . it steers and handles impeccably, it performs extremely well, and its reputation for durability and stamina is widely acclaimed by many thousands of satisfied owners. In our opinion, this truly is the 'universal' sports car."

There was just time for a final competition flourish: a 1600 De Luxe Coupe took a class win at the 12 Hours of Sebring in 1961. Ted Lund's SRX210 returned to Le Mans

Power to overtake with Safety *Power* to surmount difficulties Power in hand More Power

than ever!

THE NEW MGA '1600'

MGA 1600

with heavily modified bodywork and a 128-brake-horse-power engine, but it blew up! Luckily, a works-built 1600 MkII De Luxe Coupe (the 115-brake-horsepower 151 ABL) won its class in the 1962 Monte Carlo and Tulip rallies.

Road car production ended in the summer of 1962, with 8,719 MkIIs built. Perhaps the most staggering statistic is that the MG that Lord almost kyboshed had, in just seven years, become the world's best-selling sports car, with overall sales of 101,081, just over 80 percent of which had been exported to the USA. It had obliterated total prewar sales several times in just a single year and cemented the name MG in the consciousnesses of a new generation and all without an MG-built engine.

It surely couldn't get any better.

(Above) This MGA 1600 brochure leaves readers in no doubt as to the new car's raison d'être.

(Opposite) An MGA ad shows the now separate brake and indicator lamps on the new 1600's derriere, while tempting potential buyers with its editorial beauty.

(Above) This rear profile of the
MGA 1600 MkII is complete with
Mini-sourced horizontal rear
lamp clusters.

(Opposite) Discreet badging
denotes the final flourish for
the MGA model.

1955–1959

MGA

Models	Tourer (£595-£663), from 1956 Coupe (£699-£724)		Gearbox	4-speed manual
			Automatic	n/a
Construction	Steel chassis and body		Final Drive Ratio	4.3:1
Length	156 in (396.2 cm)		Steering	Rack and pinion
Width	57.25 in (145.4 cm)		Front Suspension	Independent by coil springs, wishbones, and lever-arm dampers
Height	50 in (127 cm)			
Wheelbase	94 in (238.76 cm)		Rear Suspension	Live axle on half-elliptic leaf springs, lever-arm dampers
Weight	Tourer 1,988 lb (901.7 kg), Coupe 2,105 lb (954.8 kg)			
			Tires	5.50 × 15 in
Engine Size	1,489cc		Brakes	Lockheed hydraulic brakes, 10.75-in (27.3 cm) drums all around
Engine Format	In-line 4-cylinder			
Carburetion	2 × 1.5-in SU carburetors		0 to 60 mph	15.6 sec
Max Bhp	68 bhp @ 5,500 rpm (72 bhp @ 5500 rpm, shortly after launch)		Top Speed	98 mph (157.7 km/h)
			Fuel Economy	27 mpg (US, 22.48 mpg)
Max Torque	78 lb-ft @ 3,000 rpm			

1959–1961

As above for MGA 1600, except

Models	Tourer (£663); Coupe (£724)		Brakes	Lockheed hydraulic brakes, 11-in (27.9 cm) front discs, 10.75-in (27.3 cm) rear drums
Weight	Tourer 2,015 lb (914 kg), Coupe 2,075 lb (941.2 kg)			
			0 to 60 mph	14.2 sec
Engine Size	1,588cc		Top Speed	101 mph (162.5 km/h)
Max Bhp	80 bhp @ 5,600 rpm		Fuel Economy	24.1 mpg (US, 20.07 mpg)
Max Torque	87 lb-ft @ 3,800 rpm			

1961–1962

As above for MGA 1600 MkII, except

Models	Tourer (£663), Coupe (£724)		Brakes	Lockheed hydraulic brakes, 11-in (27.9 cm) front discs, 10.75-in (27.3 cm) rear drums
Weight	Tourer 1,985 lb (900.4 kg), Coupe 2,045 lb (927.6 kg)			
			0 to 60 mph	12.8 sec
Engine Size	1,622cc		Top Speed	101 mph (162.5 km/h)
Max Bhp	90 bhp @ 5,500 rpm		Fuel Economy	22.3 mpg (US, 18.57 mpg)
Max Torque	97 lb-ft @ 4,000 rpm			

1958–1960

MGA Twin Cam

Models	Tourer (£843), Coupe (£904)		**Gearbox**	4-speed manual
Construction	Steel chassis and body		**Automatic**	n/a
Length	156 in (396.2 cm)		**Final Drive Ratio**	4.3:1
Width	57.25 in (145.4 cm)		**Steering**	Rack and pinion
Height	50 in (127 cm)		**Front Suspension**	Independent by coil springs, wishbones, and Armstrong lever-arm dampers
Wheelbase	91 in (231 cm)		**Rear Suspension**	Live axle on half elliptic leaf springs, Armstrong lever-arm dampers
Weight	Tourer 2,185 lb (991.1 kg), Coupe 2,245 lb (1,018.3 kg)		**Tires**	5.90 × 15 in
Engine Size	1,588cc		**Brakes**	Dunlop 10.75 in (27.3 cm) disc brakes, all around
Engine Format	In-line 4-cylinder		**0 to 60 mph**	9.1 sec
Carburetion	2 × 1.75-in SU carburetors		**Top Speed**	113 mph (181.9 km/h)
Max Bhp	108 bhp @ 6,700 rpm		**Fuel Economy**	21.8 mpg (US, 18.15 mpg)
Max Torque	104 lb-ft @ 4,500 rpm			

CHAPTER 8

A NEW SMALL CAR:
SAY HELLO TO THE "SPRIDGET"

Knowing the MGA was too pricey for some, Abingdon turned to stablemate Austin Healey to create a "new" budget sports car. The Austin-Healey Sprite and MG Midget, with their collective nickname "Spridget," sprang from the often begrudging collaboration. Competition, though, is a powerful force and, with the release of rival Triumph's Spitfire, the sub-brands discovered their team spirit.

MG brought out the historical big guns for the release of the "rubber bumper" Midget, MGB Roadster, and MGB GT.

If you're going to choose an existing vehicle on which to base your new entry-level sports car, then it goes without saying that you should choose a very good one. And that's exactly what BMC did, piggybacking the MG Midget on the Austin-Healey Sprite.

The original concept was Donald Healey's. After the success of the Austin-Healey 100, his Warwick-based concern started exploring a cheaper, more basic sports car based on Austin A35 components. Healey presented the prototype Sprite to BMC management in January 1957 and quickly got the go-ahead. Built on a production line at Abingdon, like most BMC products, the final creation was a result of a complex, multiprocess and multilocation effort.

At the Sprite's heart lay a unitary construction (in reality semiunitary, as the exterior panels were non load-bearing) of a supremely strong design, with a crossmember-braced floorpan and multiple additional strengthening structures, including deep, boxed sills, footwell boxes, and a rigid propshaft tunnel. To keep manufacturing costs tight, they constructed in steel only, with the hood and front fenders one single, rear-hinged section and a solid, rounded back end with no external luggage access.

Running gear was in the main Austin A35, with the A-Series engine endowed with twin carburetors for 43 brake horsepower. Rack and pinion steering came from the Morris Minor, the rear suspension had quarter elliptic rear springs, and its most unique feature was the pod-housed headlights, which quickly gained it the nickname "Frogeye" (or "Bug-eye," in the US).

If the Morris Motor Company had originally brought affordable motoring to the masses, then it was the £445 (£669 with purchase tax) Austin-Healey Sprite that truly opened up the world of sports car motoring to the general public. Light, strong, and immensely responsive,

(Above) A basic construction design ensured a supremely low-ticket price, but the lack of an opening trunk limited the Sprite's practicality.

(Opposite) The Austin-Healey "Frogeye" (or "Bug-eye") Sprite's cutesy styling polarized opinion and, according to Thornley, was canned just as it was starting to become accepted.

it was a challenge for anyone strapped into one to emerge without a smile. Yes, outright puff was limited, but with your bum barely skimming the tarmac, supremely direct steering and a go-cart like rear end, it was a riotous little imp and, just like big brother Healey 100, greater than the sum of its parts.

Success was instant, with 21,566 produced in 1959, but buyers weren't without their complaints. Chief amongst these were the lack of rear luggage space, the heavy combined hood/front fenders panel, and its permanent "Bambi in headlights" looks.

Despite a reduction in purchase tax that saw the total asking price reduced to £631, sales dropped to 18,648 in 1960, and BMC management decided that modifications were required. While the Healey Company redesigned the front end with Geoffrey Healey himself, who'd overseen the original Sprite project, taking on the oversight, BMC gave reimagining the rear end as a separate task to Enever at Abingdon. When the two got wind of this division of labor, they circumvented potential disaster by arranging to meet at the Morris Bodies Branch in Coventry, unbeknownst to senior management.

With both parties in conversation, the project moved on smoothly and quickly. Healey's team designed new front fenders with a separate hood hinged at the scuttle. Back in Abingdon, they added a separate, opening trunk lid and integrated rear fenders. The latter necessitated internal bracing on both wheel arches, each of which was lowered and squared off. With Enever on board, it was no surprise that the finished article closely resembled the upcoming MGB.

To compensate for the new body coming in 60 pounds (27 kg) heavier, the A-Series engine got a different camshaft,

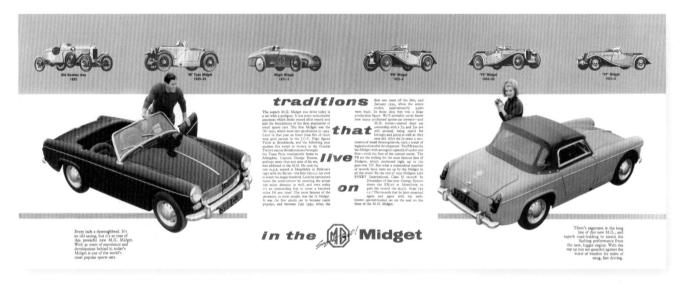

(Left) At this 1958 Abingdon factory, you can just make out the raised one-piece front clamshells of the Austin-Healey Sprites behind the MGA Twin Cam production line.

(Opposite) The new Midget bore a close resemblance to its MGB big brother—no surprise, as Enever played a key role in both designs.

larger inlet valves, and larger, 1¼-inch (3.2 cm) SU carburetors. The team also raised the compression ratio for a power output of 46.5 brake horsepower. The chassis and general running gear remained the same.

Perhaps the biggest surprise was BMC's decision, which reflected a clarity of upper management thought at a time when much that came down from on high resembled the polar opposite, to resurrect the famous "Midget" name, and market the vehicle as both an Austin-Healey and an MG. Abingdon, after all, remained synonymous with the sports car. It was enough to make MG enthusiasts (and dealers) jump for joy, if not the Donald Healey Motor Company, which received not a penny in commission for the "new" car based entirely on its initial concept.

1961–1963: BROTHERS IN ARMS

The Sprite MkII launched in June 1961 to almost universal acclaim of both its fresh clothes and newfound practicality. Rather than introduce its twin at the same time, BMC waited almost a month before revealing the new MkI Midget (the MG's model designation always ran one "Mk" behind its Austin-Healey counterpart).

In its preview, *Autocar* forgave the blatant corporate policy that had resulted in its production, and instead hailed "… the revival of one of the most honored names in the history of motorsport." The article praised the design and noted its similarities to the Sprite MkII, as well as the effort to make it an MG in its own right (including a cabin resemblance to the MGA's), before concluding, "This is perhaps most important of all, for it will give a lot of young people the chance to own a new MG."

At £669 15s 10d (including purchase tax), it was just over £38 more expensive than the Sprite and viewed right from the get-go as a "luxury version" of the Austin-Healey—this despite the fact that BMC offered the Sprite itself in standard (minus rev counter, windshield washer, and front and rear bumpers) and deluxe forms (at £655 12s 6d, much closer to the Midget's price tag).

Those opting for the MG received an Ivory-colored steering wheel, more thickly padded seats with additional contrast piping, a better-quality front floor covering (mottled plastic lined underneath with felt, rather than ribbed rubber), all-black dials, and a padded dashboard top. On the exterior, its vertical aluminum bar grille and additional chrome trim strips (on the center of the hood and down each flank) lent it a touch more visual pizzazz, working with the MG emblems to give it its own character.

A long line of optional extras included a heater and demister, radio, tonneau cover, Ace Mercury wheel discs, luggage rack, whitewall tires, Dunlop Fort tires, rear compartment cushion, locking petrol cap, laminated windshield, twin horns, and a low-compression (8.3:1) engine. Perversely, in an era of cost saving, and on a model derived for that very same reason, the optional fiberglass hardtop for each car was of a different design.

The first road tests were unequivocally positive, with general praise for the smoothness of the engine,

close-ratios of the gearbox and precise nature of the steering—with only the stopping power thought by some to be a little lacking.

0 to 60 miles per hour was generally measured at 18 to 20 seconds, with a top speed of 86 miles per hour (138 km/h), all while returning a combined 33 miles per gallon. Owners could expect a high level of frugality for their sporting kicks. In that first year, the Midget sold 7,656 units, compared to 10,064 Sprites—in combination not quite the total number of Sprites from the previous year, but better followed.

With the arrival of the MGB and BMC's new front-wheel-drive Mini derivatives, 1962 was a busy year. The Spridgets' change to a 1,098cc engine, as fitted in the Morris 1100 model, could almost have passed without notice—especially as BMC never gave it an official designation. Power rose to 56 brake horsepower, with a corresponding 0 to 60-miles-per-hour time of 17 seconds and a top speed of 89 miles per hour (143 km/h). The

(Top left) The MG wore a vertical bar grille (rather than the Sprite's egg-crate item) and, compared to its sibling, was complemented by several extra trim items, including the central hood strip.

(Bottom left) The biggest change for both new cars was the addition of an opening trunk lid. Up front, note the identical interior fascia to the MkII Sprite's, but with a white rather than black steering wheel.

(Opposite top) Less basic than the MkI Sprite certainly, but sidescreens remained the go-to weatherproofing method; wire wheels were not initially an option.

THE JACOBS RACING COUPES

Happenstance certainly played a key part in the development of the diminutive racing coupes. Ex-MG racer, and then MG dealer, Dick Jacobs was in the office of his North East London-based Mill Garage dealership, poring over a side profile in the catalog for the upcoming Midget. Also open on the desk was a *Motor* magazine road test of an Aston Martin DB4. Using a piece of tracing paper, he quickly transposed the Aston's roofline over the MG and hey presto, the coupe idea was born.

Thornley and Enever were immediately enthused by Jacobs' vision of a small-capacity GT competition car, and the works department set to building three examples that would be loaned to, and run by, Jacobs.

Using a standard steel floorpan, Enever designed the bumperless alloy body to incorporate a significantly reshaped, more aerodynamic nose. Suspension remained standard save for stiffer dampers. In came disc brakes, and they bored out the engine to 979cc and fitted it with a Weber 45 DCOE carburetor. Weighing just 1,232 lb (559 kg) and with a power output of 75 brake horsepower, it was a feisty little tyke capable of a top speed of 120 mph (193 km/h), despite a reasonably tame state of tune chosen with one eye on long-distance race reliability.

Just three examples were built—770 BJB and 771 BJB going to Jacobs and 138 DJB to John Milne in Scotland. They were competitive from the start, scoring multiple victories in

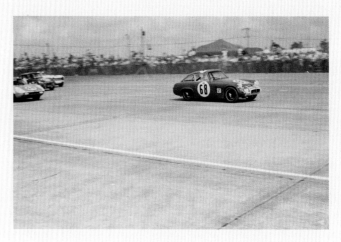

The "Jacobs" Midget of Andrew Hedges and Roger Mac streaks ahead of the competition on the 1965 12 Hours of Sebring, on its way to a first in class win.

the up-to-1,000cc category, even more so after a rejig fitted them with ZF differentials, softer rear springs, special bushes, and Aeon rubber bump stops.

Bigger engines arrived—1,098cc in '62/'63, and 1,239cc in 1964—before the Jacobs cars came "home" in late 1964, to be run by the BMC works team. Perhaps their greatest success came at that year's 12 Hours of Sebring (until that point more synonymous with the Sprite), where Andrew Hedges and Roger Mac romped to first in Class in 771 BJB.

The MkI's Austin-designed A-Series engine (now up-rated to 46.5 bhp) provided the oomph for both Austin-Healey and MG "Spridget" variants.

gearbox switched from cone-type synchromesh to a stronger baulk-ring design—although first gear was still nonsynchro—and 8.25-inch (210 mm) Lockheed front disc brakes significantly upgraded stopping power. Interior quality of both models improved. Cabins were now fully carpeted, Smiths gauges standardized, and an electronic rev counter fitted—with just a £23 rise in asking price.

The arrival of Standard-Triumph's Triumph Spitfire in October of that year changed everything—suddenly, there was a serious new rival in town.

Faster, roomier, and with more modern accoutrements (albeit more expensive and not as sweet handling), by the end of 1963 it had comprehensively outsold the BMC cars, shifting 20,950 units to the Spridgets' combined 16,477.

Something had to be done.

1964–1965: LIKE BEFORE, BUT BETTER

In light of the Spitfire, the MkII Midget/MkIII Sprite required a distinct rethink to make them more practical. Focus fell on comfort and convenience. The sidescreens were ditched in favor of wind-up windows, and proper locking external and internal handles replaced the earlier metal lever releases. Incorporating them and opening quarter lights in the minute doors was

(Above) MkII, a triumph of packaging, saw the arrival of wind-up windows. Note the door-opening mechanism positioned at the extreme edge of the door.

(Below) A photo of the interior shows new fascia, although combined here with an aftermarket steering wheel, opening quarter lights, and bulkier windshield frame.

MORE BADGE ENGINEERING

Based on the ADO16 range, the MG 1100, released in 1962, was the first ever Abingdon product with front-wheel drive and a transversely mounted engine.

Basking in the glow of Alec Issogonis's Mini, his understudy Charles Griffin had designed a new, slightly larger car to an almost identical formula. The result was a similarly tightly packaged product, with an overly generous cabin—perfect as a small, family buzzbox.

Unsurprisingly, power came via the A-Series engine in 1,098cc form. It did differ in the suspension layout, with the first introduction of Dr. Alex Moulton's innovative all-independent Hydrolastic design. To improve ride quality, the 1100 kept the floorpan level at all the times, thanks to its interconnected front-to-rear spheres (rubber casings with water). The result was a smooth, even ride, but one that many found a little disconcerting, with its tendency to make the occupants feel as though they were floating above the road surface.

Also, as per the times, those buying the MG version received twin carburetors (for 55 brake horsepower rather than all other variants' 48 brake horsepower), a different fascia, and plusher trim. On the exterior, just as with the MkIII and IV Magnettes, it was the badging and grille that marked it as different from its siblings.

Available initially only as a four-door model, it received a lukewarm response. In December 1962, *Autocar*—while having some minor criticisms—concluded, "Fundamentally the MG 1100 is difficult to fault, and our liking for it never wavered throughout the test," and that it was, "a very worthy wearer of the octagon."

Like the Mini, it was a perky and decent-handling little car and sold accordingly, with 26,404 finding a home in '63 and 32,703 the following year. A two-door, and even a three-door Estate model, soon became available, and you could even have a luxury "Vanden Plas Princess 1100" version, complete with picnic tables—advertised as the MG Princess 1100 in the US.

In spring 1967 the 1100 body shell received a 1,275cc version of the engine, with single carburetor and 58 brake horsepower. Then in autumn the MG 1300 arrived, coinciding with a general facelift (and the availability of an AP four-speed automatic transmission).

The 1100 was quickly dropped, leaving the 1300 MkII, with its 70 brake horsepower engine as the only option. By 1971 this new MG "Sports Sedan" had sold a very decent 157,409 examples, with just over half being exported.

MG-1100
Safety fast!

The M.G. 1100 utilises the most advanced engineering technique to pack high performance, comfort, safety and spaciousness into a stylish car of compact dimensions.

(Left) *This ad combines a peculiar juxtaposition of the model's upright traditional lines and the beach cool of sixties America.*

(Opposite) *This 1966* Motor Trend *test car was marketed as the two-door "MG Sports Sedan." Twin carburetors, two-tone paintwork, and an up-market interior differentiated the MG from its Austin and Morris brethren.*

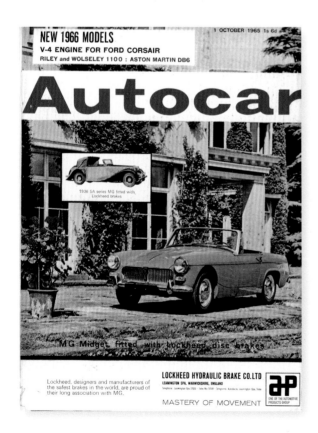

no mean feat, managed by locating the internal units right at the very rear edge of structure; a new windshield design was incorporated to mate to the new quarter lights and wind-up windows. The door pockets were also lost, but a small parcel shelf under the nearside fascia offset this. The dashboard housing itself was now a black steel pressing finished in crackle black, with the speedometer and tachometer set in an angled housing. An MGB-type steering wheel was also added. Up top, the hood now had a rigid front rail that could be clipped in place to the new deeper windshield surround—although, along with the frame, it still needed to be removed completely and stored in the trunk. Still, now being better weatherproofed, the Spridgets were now a better daily driver option.

Engineers strengthened the engine's bottom end (seen as something of a weakness on the 1,098cc unit), fitted the MG 1100 cylinder head, added a new exhaust manifold, and replaced the old mechanical fuel pump with an SU electric unit. Power rose accordingly to 59 brake horsepower at 5,750 rpm and torque to 65 pound-feet at 3,500 rpm, bringing the 0 to 60-miles-per-hour sprint time to 14.5 seconds.

The biggest change came at the rear end, where a more compliant, half-elliptic leaf spring system replaced the quarter-elliptic leaf spring/radius arm setup. Stiffening the rear end for the Mk1 Sprite transition to MKII Sprite/MkI Midget meant that it was no longer necessary to feed the rear suspension stresses into the floorpan. And with better axle location, they could fit softer springs to endow the car with a less harsh ride while at the same time further improving the handling.

The changes were well received and in 1964 sales of both models rose accordingly (it was the first year that the Midget numbers just surpassed those of its BMC sibling). Their combined sales climbed to less than a thousand behind the Spitfire's total—although they'd fall further behind again, in 1965.

That year in the US, BMC raced two works Midgets at the American Bridgehampton Double 500 meeting. These weren't the famed Jacobs' cars, rather a separate

pair purpose-built at the behest of Comps boss Stuart Turner. The meeting counted towards the FIA World Championship of Makes for GT cars. BMC felt it was key that they resemble their production brethren, so there was no special aerodynamic bodywork, just lightweight alloy panels and a 1,293cc Mini Cooper S A-Series engine for an estimated power output just north of 100 brake horsepower.

The efforts were worth it. Rauno Aaltonen powered his British Racing Green MkII to a class win (sixth overall), and MG took second place in the 1,300cc class of the GT Constructors Championship.

These were the last works efforts, although privately run Midgets won their class in the Sports Car Club of America (SCCA) racing championships of 1966 and 1970.

1966–1970: THREE IS THE MAGIC NUMBER

The Spitfire–Spridget war saw a series of tit-for-tat improvements from each manufacturer. BMC introduced the 1,275cc A-Series from the Mini Cooper S into the MkIII Midget/MkIV Sprite . . . sort of. Redesigned for ease of (and cheaper) production, they lowered the compression ratio from 9.5:1 to 8.8:1, fitted smaller cylinder head valves, and ditched the Nitralloy crankshaft for a lower-spec item. Even given this, it was still good for 65 brake horsepower (11 brake horsepower less than in the Cooper S) and a 16-percent torque increase. BMC coupled this with a new permanent hood frame, one that was simple to use and easily stowed.

Triumph responded with its 75-brake-horsepower Spitfire MkIII and the rivals went to battle once more. Pitting a Midget III versus a Spitfire MkIII, in September

1967, *Road and Track* weighed the pros and cons of each carefully, before diplomatically declaring it a dead heat—"But whichever the buyer chooses, he is assured of many miles of motoring pleasure in the great sports car tradition. They're good cars, both of them. You can't go wrong,"—although it did note that for a comparative spec, the MG was $200 cheaper.

In 1968, the financial issues that had dogged BMC for a number of years forced a merger with the Leyland Motor Corporation Ltd. Incredibly, MG now found itself under the same British Leyland Motor Corporation banner as Triumph. Worse still, with Leyland the senior partner (and Triumph-centric Donald Stokes at the helm), MG was now firmly down the pecking order.

To meet new Federal emissions laws, US market cars received the first of what became a series of detuned engines giving 62 brake horsepower, as well as dual-circuit brakes and three-point seat belts. In the UK, twin reversing lights and negative earth electrics were introduced. A heater was now standard, and most vehicles had an oil cooler and a front anti-roll bar.

In early 1969, they fitted a 3.9:1-ratio rear axle, with reclining seats arriving later in the year. By year end, combined Spridget sales outstripped the Spitfire's for the first time: 6,136 Sprite MkIVs and 12,965 Midget MkIIIs sold, compared to 18,574 Triumphs. This was a blip, as normal service resumed the year after and stayed for the remainder of their rivalry.

British Leyland had a modernization drive in 1970, with a new black "egg-crate" radiator grill (far more successful than that of big brother, the MGB) and satin black sills with chrome Midget (or, for the Austin-Healey, Sprite) lettering, British Leyland badges on the lower fenders by each door, and slimmer bumpers sporting overriders with rubber inserts.

The Midget's chrome side strips joined the hood item that had departed the previous year. The windshields and quarter lights now had an anodized matte Black finish (although this proved unpopular and was quickly dropped in favor of anodized aluminum), and the interior trim was updated. Lastly a whole host of funky seventies British Leyland colors (with

The British Leyland facelift included a new egg-crate grille with a center-mounted badge and chrome surrounding strip.

names such as Bronze Yellow, Harvest Gold, Bracken, Tundra, Mirage, and Bedouin) were offered.

It was the end of an era at Abingdon, with General Manager Thornley—so long the driving force—retiring early due to ill health. Another stalwart, Enever, would join him within two years.

To Donald Stokes, paying a royalty on a car when there was an identical one being produced in-house must have seemed like madness; so, in 1970 he cancelled the company's association with the famous Healey name.

1971–1973: AND THEN THERE WAS ONE

For January 1971 the company renamed the Austin-Healey Sprite as the Austin Sprite, and it was the same in every way except for some new badges. However, the reality was that there was now no benefit to having two doppelgangers (save the aesthetic differences) for sale and they pulled the Austin by summer.

With the master gone, the apprentice now had the field to itself—achieving an all-time best annual sales figure of 16,469. In truth though, that was just a little under 1500 more than the previous year—the reality was Stokes's call was the right one as the Austin-Healey Sprite had run its course (sales in 1970 had been a paltry 1,282—down almost 5k from the previous year).

In October 1971 *Motor Trend* acknowledged the aged design's limitations (and that of the MGB), while still praising its underlying nature, ". . .blunt, strong and by today's standards of sophistication, almost crude, they accomplish their purpose. . . in a manner both surprising and admirable".

For 1972, and for the first time since the original Sprite, designers resurrected round rear-wheel arches. New Rostyle wheels—with their distinctive cloverleaf

(Above) Rostyle wheels and matte black sills with Midget badges completed the fresh new look.

(Right) Badges at the rear of the base of each front wing signified the new corporate ownership of the MG brand.

(Opposite) The MkIII featured a redesigned rear deck with a fold-down top that was much easier to use. Round rear wheelarches wouldn't arrive until 1973.

design—came in, as did an alternator in place of the original dynamo, while US engines saw a return to a lower 8.0:1 compression ratio. In the UK, at £1,003, the Midget asking price crossed the psychological £1,000 barrier for the first time.

The following year saw the Midget pulled from all other markets except for the US (where over 75 percent were still exported) and UK. Other changes were minimal with 145-13 radial tires standardized for both countries, and Navy Blue and Ochre now the interior trim choices (although these only lasted a year before there was return to their predecessors).

The Midget, while still immensely fun to drive, was beginning to look a little old hat compared to recent and more sophisticated arrivals on the small sports car scene. And yet, there still remained no sign of a replacement on the horizon.

1974–1979: THE FINAL COUNTDOWN

As British Leyland lurched between crises—some out of it control, others of its own making—and reshaped itself, first (after its collapse and nationalization) as Leyland Cars and then British Leyland Cars, sales of the Midget held their course.

In 1974, new US safety legislation prompted the company to add large rubber overriders, and then Marley Polyurethane "rubber" bumpers appeared on the Midget 1500. Square rear arches returned at the same time for extra strength. These changes added 167.6 pounds (76 kg) and a raised ride height, which negatively impacted handling. None of it seemed to impact vehicle sales. In fact, sales jumped by almost 2k in 1975 and over another 2k in '76, to an all-time high of 16,879, but the fitting of a Triumph engine may have helped.

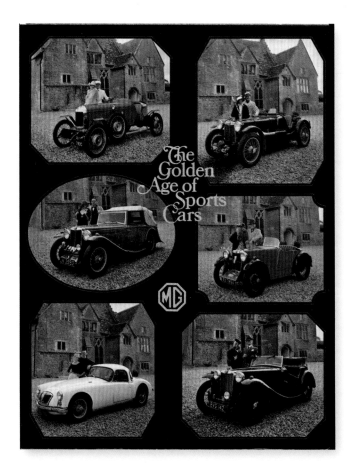

The use of highly successful models of yesteryear perhaps only served to emphasize that the new car didn't look at all like them (certainly compared to the chrome-bumpered MGA).

THE CONVERTORS

From the word go the original Frogeye Sprite saw the converters and improvers get to work. John Sprinzel of Speedwell offered the "Speedwell Sprite," with 1½" (3.81 cm) carburetors, a polished cylinder head, 8.7:1 compression ratio, and 50 brake horsepower. In 1961, after he had left Speedwell, his Sebring Sprites came in a dizzying six stages of tune—the hairiest being the 87-brake-horsepower supercharged version.

Shorrock A-Series supercharger kits (£82, including fitting) were also popular, and the usual tuning suspects, such as Downton, offered their take on things. Ashley Laminates Ltd was among numerous outfits providing lightweight fiberglass hoods and hardtops.

With the advent of the Midget, the sheer range of offerings only increased. In 1963, for the price of £250, Speedwell added new pistons, a special crankshaft, a lightweight flywheel, a new camshaft, a light alloy cylinder head, and a twin-choke Weber 45 DCOE carburetor to create their 1,098cc "Clubman 85" spec Speedwell Midget. The alterations produced a lofty 89 brake horsepower at 7,000 rpm and 78 lb-ft at 5,500 rpm of torque. Buyers could further amp up this little lightning bolt by adding an aerodynamic "Monza" hood (£49, 10s) and a "Clubman" hardtop (£37, 10s). 0 to 60 mph in 9.1 sec and a dizzying top speed of 105.8 mph, anyone?

Of course, you didn't need to go quite that far. London-based Taurus Performance Tuning Ltd would mildly tweak your 948cc Midget for just £74, 10s. Its "Stage 1" Taurus cylinder head, twin 1½ SU carburetors on a new manifold, and special camshaft were enough to make it considerably faster than its larger, 1,098cc-engined sibling.

Perhaps the best-known modification specialist was Kent-based Lenham Motor Company. Its Lenham GT was a fixed-head version, that turned the MkI Sprite into a closed coupe with a steeply raked rear window and Kamm-type tail. This was a fairly drastic conversion that removed the rear fenders and panels and bonded a new fiberglass Lenham-designed section in place—and as such, it was irreversible. With the 1964 arrival of the new Spridgets, this morphed into the Lenham Le Mans Coupe, which now incorporated rear quarter windows at each side. There was even the option of an open GTO version.

For the MKIII Midget, Bedford-based Car Preparations' Atlantis 1600 involved (a bridge too far, perhaps) a conversion to Ford crossflow 1.6-liter power. From the start, MG's sports car output had leant themselves well to tweaking, improvement, and tuning, but never had a model seen such a dizzying array of embellishments as the postwar Midget.

A Lenham Midget in full flow; its Kamm-tail fastback style proved popular but was irreversible once a significant proportion of the donor car's rear end had been cut out.

Yes, you read that right. To offset power loss due to strangling US smog equipment, Triumph had, in 1973, fitted a de-tuned 1,493cc engine to its Spitfire. With no room to increase the A-Series unit's capacity, the hierarchy—in the ultimate rude salute to Abingdon employees—made the ignominious decision to fit that to the Midget as well.

If ever a decision smacked of corporate complacency, it was this. While all British Leyland's focus was on its great white hope—the Triumph—the company left the MG brand to coast, kept alive (by any means necessary) due to demand.

Perversely, it was the fastest Midget yet. With 65 brake horsepower at 5,500 rpm and 77 pound-feet torque at 3,000 rpm, it was a genuine 100-miles-per-hour (160.1 km/h) car, reaching 0 to 60 miles per hour at a touch over 12 seconds. But it was now twitchier, prone to oversteer, significantly undergeared, and its new,

(Above) Oh, the ignominy, a Triumph engine under the hood of an MG! Performance was up, but handling prowess most definitely down.

(Opposite) The Midget 1500 saw the return of square wheelarches, their additional strength required for the mounting of significantly heavier bumpers.

Morris Marina–sourced, four-speed gearbox had lost the original's snappy shift quality.

Out in the US, a reduced 7.5:1 compression ratio and single Zenith carburetor saw it produce an asthmatic 50 brake horsepower at 5,000 rpm and 67 pound-feet torque. Top speed was 85 miles per hour (140 km/h), and 0 to 60 miles per hour was over two seconds slower than the UK variant.

Changes over the next few years were few and far between. Headrests became standard in '77. In 1979, the manufacturer switched it to a 3.72:1 rear axle ratio and made dual-circuit braking standard in the UK.

By this point goodwill was fast departing, and attitudes towards the once-admired vehicle had changed. "Why on earth would anyone want one?" asked a *Road & Track* special, while *Car and Driver* cited a clear lack of any development: "The Midget simply isn't a serious car anymore."

The latter half of the 1970s brought a genuine success story to a rather inglorious end. The last 500 Midgets produced wore Black, with commemorative plaques that read "1929–1979—Fifty years of the MG Midget." The final car rolled off the production line in November 1979. The Midget (and its Sprite counterpart) had offered generation after generation at home and around the world an introduction to cheap, simple, perky, smile-inducing sports car motoring.

And they still do.

1961–1964
Midget MkI

Models	Roadster (£472)	Gearbox	4-speed manual
Construction	Steel unit-construction body/chassis	Automatic	n/a
Length	136.25 in (346 cm)	Final Drive Ratio	4.22:1
Width	53.9 in (137 cm)	Steering	Rack and pinion
Height	49.8 in (126.4 cm)	Front Suspension	Independent by coil springs, wishbones, hydraulic lever-arm dampers
Wheelbase	80 in (203.2 cm)		
Weight	1,572 lb (713 kg)	Rear Suspension	Beam axle on quarter-elliptic leaf springs, radius arms, hydraulic lever-arm dampers
Engine Size	948cc		
Engine Format	In-line 4-cylinder		
Carburetion	2 × SU HS2 carburetors	Tires	5.20 × 13 in
Max Bhp	46.5 bhp @ 5,500 rpm	Brakes	Front drums (discs from 1962), rear drums
Max Torque	52.5 lb-ft @ 2,750 rpm		
		0 to 60 mph	18.3 sec
		Top Speed	86 mph (138 km/h)
		Fuel Economy	33 mpg (US, 27.5 mpg)

1961–1964

As above for 1,098cc Midget MkI, except

Models	Roadster (£495)
Engine Size	1,098cc
Max Bhp	55 bhp @ 5,750 rpm

0 to 60 mph	17.0 sec
Top Speed	89 mph (143 km/h)

1964–1966

As above for 1,098cc Midget MkII, except

Models	Roadster (£505)
Engine Size	1,098cc
Max Bhp	59 bhp @ 5,750 rpm

0 to 60 mph	14.5 sec
Top Speed	92 mph (148 km/h)

1964–1974

As above for 1,275cc Midget MkIII, except

Models	Roadster (£555-£1,103)
Engine Size	1,275cc
Engine Format	In-line 4-cylinder
Max Bhp	65 bhp @ 6,000 rpm
Rear Suspension	Beam axle on half-elliptic leaf springs, radius arms, hydraulic lever-arm dampers

Final Drive Ratio	4.22:1, later 3.9:1
Brakes	Front drums (discs from 1962), rear drums
0 to 60 mph	14.0 sec
Top Speed	93.5 mph (150.5 km/h)

1974–1979

As above for Midget 1500, except

Models	Roadster (£1,351-£2,802)
Engine Size	1,493cc
Length	141 in (358 cm)
Front Suspension	Independent by coil springs, wishbones, hydraulic lever-arm dampers, anti-roll bar

Rear Suspension	Live axle on half-elliptic leaf springs, radius arms, hydraulic lever-arm dampers
Tires	145/13
Max Bhp	66 bhp @ 5,500 rpm
0 to 60 mph	12.2 sec
Top Speed	101 mph (161 km/h)

As above for Midget 1500 Federal Market car, except

Max Bhp	50 bhp @ 5,000 rpm
0 to 60 mph	16.3 sec
Top Speed	86 mph (138.4 km/h)

CHAPTER 9

MGB:

THE KING IS DEAD, LONG LIVE THE KING!

Having struck gold with the MGA, MG found a new vein with its replacement. Utilizing contemporary production methods, they created a modern take on the MGA. Not only did this new automobile outsell its predecessor, but—in chrome and 'rubber' bumper forms—it lasted an incredible eighteen years in production, all with the most minimal of mechanical and styling revisions.

The 1974½ facelift saw the arrival of the US federal safety legislation–induced polyurethane "rubber bumpers," prolonging the MGB's North American life cycle.

Considerations for an updated MGA began as early as 1957, with the Italian Carrozzeria Frua commissioned to design a body for an experimental prototype (codenamed EX214). Compared to the elegant lines normally astride the donor chassis, the proposal certainly had a touch more Latin brio—looking to some far more Maserati, than MG. But with styling, cost, and weight considerations, MG swiftly deemed this avenue a dead end.

Instead MG decided to pursue an outright replacement. Codenamed EX205, the MGB (could it ever have had any other name?) project opted for a new unitary construction structure over the traditional chassis-body arrangement. While the hope was that this would increase strength and decrease weight, cost also increased. Pressed Steel's initial outlay for tooling was enough to make even the most generous of BMC's bean-counter's eyes water. Arch negotiator Thornley haggled a deal that appeared surreptitiously lower on paper while being in reality offset by a higher price per completed body. The

Morris Bodies Branch Factory in Coventry assembled each using the Pressed Steel–provided floorpan and panel sets, painted them, then sent them to Abingdon for final assembly.

Frua's wasn't the only styling attempt made for the MGB. MG's Don Hayter based his on an MGA chassis, including a design for a fixed-head coupe. Using his soft-top sketch as a basis, he slowly evolved the new car's lines. Its initial MGA-style sloping hood gave way to a more upright style, all the better for a larger radiator and perhaps a longer and larger engine. He reduced its wheelbase to 7 feet 7 inches (2.3 m)—3 inches (7.6 cm) shorter than that of its predecessor. The company quickly approved his final design—modern, elegant, and more spacious inside—bore a close resemblance to the new upright lines of the Midget.

Given the go-ahead, and internal moniker ADO 23, work now turned to mechanical specification. Chief Engineer Enever's team decided to continue with the same independent front suspension—traceable all the way back to the YA—and live axle and leaf-spring location setup as its MGA predecessor, although the new car did receive a higher-ratio 3.909:1 rear axle, as well as softer spring and damper settings.

The gearbox remained the sweet-shifting, close-ratio four-speed (nonsynchromesh in first) MGA unit, with Laycock overdrive coming in as an option. On the engine front, the team gave consideration first to a V-4 engine and then, the MGA 1600 MkII's 1,622cc overhead-valve B-Series unit.

In the end the threat of the new model having no real performance improvement over the old (never a good look for an automobile manufacturer) saw the team bring forward an updated 1,798cc version of the B-Series that had been in development. The capacity was upped by increasing the bore. That, alongside new pistons with concave crowns, resulted in a healthy 95 brake horsepower and 110 pound-feet of torque—a respectable leap from 86 brake horsepower and 97 pound-feet. An oil cooler sitting just in front of the radiator (an option in the UK until 1964) dealt with higher oil temperatures, and it had a removable front suspension crossmember.

The then upcoming BBC television program *Doctor Who* would no doubt also have been in planning around this same time, and the TARDIS-esque work conducted inside the car would have impressed the Time Lord himself. Despite that shorter wheelbase, the new construction method allowed the driver's pedals to be shifted forward 6 inches (15.24 cm), ensuring a significantly easier welcome for long-legged drivers. A 2-inch (5 cm) increase in width complemented this, seats were set lower in the cabin and at the rear, and a significantly bigger trunk all contributed to the impression of being "bigger on the inside." For the first time on an open-top MG, winding windows—a modern convenience, but anathema for aficionados of earlier Octagon wares—replaced sidescreens.

Although mechanically very similar to its outgoing relation, the new MGB had a smart, fresh look clothing

(Above) MkI MGB Roadsters on the Abingdon production line; the company built 4,518 in 1962 and a lofty 23,308 the following year.

(Opposite) Frua's EX214 took definite styling cues from the Maserati 3500GT Spyder, but MG rejected it in favor of an in-house design.

its strong monocoque structure, a significantly roomier interior, and a decent performance boost. Time to see what the motoring public and press thought. . .

1962–1964: A NEW ERA

The goodwill and appetite for MG in its biggest market—North America—remained abundantly clear, and first impressions of the MGB augured well for the future: ". . . frankly this is the first British car in several years which created no arguments among the staff," declared *Road & Track* about both its styling and driving impressions. The article enthused, "This is the best engineered, best put-together MG we've ever seen."

Over in the less-affluent UK, where it was as likely to be the only car, rather than a secondary toy for a sizeable proportion of owners, there was no doubt that many of the new features—softer suspension setup, optional folding hood, and larger, more comfortable cabin—helped increase its desirability as a daily driver.

This was something *Motor* picked up on, describing the suspension as "A fine compromise between the needs for sports car firmness and the superior comfort to be expected from this much improved car . . .," and further stating, "It is obvious that a great deal of work has gone into the design of bad weather equipment for this more refined model." In summary, it found the MGB to be, "an altogether superior car to its predecessor."

Performance improvements were enough to offset coming in a touch heavier than the MGA. It whipped 1.5 seconds off the MkII 1600 MGA's 0 to 60-miles-per-hour sprint time, achieving it in 12.2 seconds, and added a couple of miles per hour to the top speed differential. It was small change but important in both sales spiel and owner bragging rights. And even with its softer feel, it still had the trademark MG handling passed on through the DNA of its illustrious sporting forebears.

Unsurprisingly there were a number of grumblings regarding the company's deviation from that out-and-out sporting heritage, with accusations that the B was

more tourer than sports car. However, in its February 1963 issue, *Cars Illustrated* suggested "The days of riding on (as opposed to 'in') hurdle-like suspension, wide open to the elements, with rough, noisy engine, and sparse creature comforts have gone." Accordingly, the B was "... a sports car in the modern manner."

At launch, the MGB retailed in the UK for £690 (£950 15s 3d, after tax), which positioned it well in the market. Rivals, such as the Triumph TR4 (£750) and Sunbeam Alpine (£695), that had struggled to compete with the MGA's impressive sales figures continued to do so with Abingdon's new and improved steed.

The numerous desirable options available included the folding roof, a heater, a full tonneau cover, an oil cooler (standard in the US), a front-anti-roll bar, spot lights, and wire wheels. A detachable hardtop followed within two months of release. Unlike most other manufacturers, MG's Competition Department made their high-performance wares available to all. If you wished—and could pay—to have your car converted to full Le Mans race car specification, you could do so.

Whatever the feelings at Abingdon prior to launch— quiet confidence or mild uneasiness—the end-of-year production figure of 4,518 was a good start. In 1963, the only production change was the January availability of a Laycock overdrive option allowing for more refined high-speed cruising. With 23,308 MGBs constructed, it didn't quite reach the MGA's best year total of 23,319 in 1959, but even better was to come the following year.

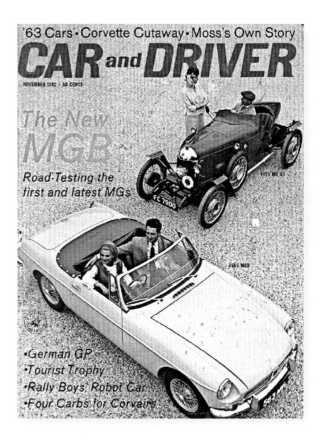

In early 1964 the original 18G version of the 1,798cc engine gave way to the 18GA closed-circuit crankcase breathing unit. When BMC introduced the Austin 1800 with its five main–bearing engine, this became the standard and the MGB received the new cylinder block from Chassis No. 46766 onwards. Other changes included replacing the original mechanically driven tachometer with a new electric unit and the oil cooler now coming as standard across the board.

(Above) After the runaway successes of the T-Type Midgets and MGA, the arrival of a new MG sports car was big news, and the US motoring press cleared their front pages accordingly.

(Left) This promotional shot of a 1962 MkI Roadster has it sitting in front of a BOAC passenger plane. Next stop the U.S. of A.?

(Opposite) Unitary construction significantly improved cabin space compared to the outgoing MGA—no room for plus-2 seats though.

A rear three-quarter profile shows elegant lines. A colored hood was available on early cars (later it was black only). Wheels are steel with chromed hubcaps rather than optional wire wheels.

1965–1966: FAMILY TIES

The early months of the new year saw the introduction of a 12-gallon (55-liter) gas tank and push-button type exterior door handles. The big news for 1965, of course, was the release of the closed-roof GT.

Sharing many panels with its soft-top progenitor, the design was initiated at Abingdon before being sent to BMC's Italian styling consultant Pininfarina for fine detailing. The result was one very graceful and rakish-looking fastback coupe—with definite echoes of the Aston Martin DB2-4, a car that had admirers within MG.

The body featured a taller windshield and window glass, with a lifting tailgate at the rear that opened to reveal a reasonably sized area for stowing luggage. The cabin was more comfortable and better appointed than the tourer, with an occasional rear seat that could be folded forward for additional storage room, incorporated by modifying the floorpan. There was no doubt about it, MG's sports car had gone over to the dark side.

In its February prerelease road test, *Motor* stated that the inevitable family man, "Stork forces sale of MG" advertisements in the automobile classifieds became a thing of the past thanks to the new model, even suggesting, "Many 'elderly ex-MG owners will be tempted to throw off their marital sedan car chains."

On the road, thanks to the GT's up-rated seven leaf rear springs, standard anti-roll bar, and more robust (and quieter) Salisbury rear axle, the magazine found that the model's "taut, rigid structure" made long journeys effortless, fully justifying its GT title.

All this practicality and refinement meant a weight increase of 159.6 pounds (72.4 kg), which somewhat blunted performance figures—adding 1.4 seconds to the 0 to 60-miles-per-hour time and reducing top speed by 2 miles per hour.

That didn't seem to matter when it launched to a strong reception at the 1965 London Motor Show. To say it sated a need in the market was an understatement; a

THE COUNE MGB BERLINETTE 1800

Contrary to public perception, the factory MGB GT wasn't the first tin-top example of the breed. In 1964, Brussels-based coachbuilder Jacques Coune released his bespoke take on a closed-cabin MGB.

Its radically revised body included reworked front fenders with headlamps further recessed and now sitting under Perspex covers; new, steeply raked front and rear windshields; fresh door glass; and a radically restyled rear end. Of course, its raison d'être was the incorporation of a fixed, full-length roof. The first six examples were completed all in steel, but the hideously expensive process soon saw that shelved for a fiberglass roof structure.

The result was an intriguing and pretty car, Italianette in style as befitted its "Berlinette" model moniker, with a luxurious, leather-trimmed interior. Its rear end, incorporating round taillights sourced from a Simca 1000 and a discreet Kamm tail, was particularly pleasant and reminiscent of a Ferrari 275GTB. The front end was a little less well resolved, with the over-high windshield lending it somewhat of a raised eyebrow aesthetic.

Despite being expensive, Counes' car sold 50 examples. Walter Oldfield, managing director of Nuffield Press, ordered

The body constructed by Jacques Coune's Brussels-based concern took the MGB to an entirely different visual place. It was largely satisfying and most definitely Italian in flavor.

and sent a standard Tartan Tourer to Belgium for conversion in April 1964. On its UK return, it was registered CWB 55B and considered by Alec Issigonis and George Harriman of BMC as a possible production variant, but its overtly Italian-influenced styling was eventually rejected in favor of Syd Enever's Pininfarina-influenced factory GT project. Its discreet lines had a much closer resemblance to its open-topped variant.

Evocative "Kamm" tail styling lent the rear of the Berlinette an aesthetic that was more Maranello than Abingdon.

RACING VERSATILITY

Nothing sums up the abilities of the BMC works racing MGBs quite like 1963–64. Three cars—6 DBL, 7 DBL, and 8 DBL—were constructed in 1963. 6 DBL and 7 DBL saw their first action in a highly unsuccessful 12 Hours of Sebring, in which both retired due to oil surge and cooling issues.

7 DBL had better luck with a class win in the sports car race at the Silverstone *Daily Express* meeting, before the team prepped it for the 24 Hours of Le Mans race. This involved fitment of a unique extended and lower nose (similar to those of the Jacobs Midgets), smoothed out for better airflow; removal of bumpers; and incorporation of Perspex headlight covers. In went a second fuel tank and a high-ratio rear axle that allowed it to hit 140 mph on the Mulsanne Straight.

Despite the disadvantage of its monocoque construction (Appendix J regulations permitted the fitting of lightweight exterior panels), it performed with aplomb, lapping at 105 mph and finishing twelfth overall and second in class at the hands of Alan Hutcheson and Paddy Hopkirk.

In 1964, 7 DBL raced again, this time in an entirely different field: the Monte Carlo Rally. Incongruous as it seems, BMC's racers were expected to compete in such disparate events as these. The discipline mattered not though, as the Morley twins (Donald and Erle) piloted the vehicle to a superb victory in the GT category (woolly governing rules allowed the MGB to run in GT classes with the detachable hardtop in place).

The strength of the racing 'Bs lay in their relative simplicity. BMC wanted its competition cars to closely resemble their production brethren, so their development was limited. While that put them at a disadvantage compared to more highly developed and powerful rivals—not necessarily a bad thing, as a giant-killing headline certainly carried more kudos—it played to the model's inherent strengths in terms of handling and reliability.

In race trim, with a single side-draft twin-choke Weber 45 DCOE carburetor, competition inlet manifold and tubular exhaust manifold, racing engines generally put out in the order of 130 brake horsepower. Couple that with a close-ratio gearbox and chassis tweaks and a racing B was a car that its rivals underestimated at their peril.

(Above) *Beauty and the Beast: Donald and Earle Morley's MGB holds off Jo Schlesser and C. Leguezec's Ford Falcon Sprint on the 1964 Monte Carlo Rally.*

(Opposite) *DRX 255C sports the unique aerodynamic nosecone first used by 7 DBL at the 24 Hours of Le Man in 1963, which it subsequently inherited to use there.*

staggering 21,835 MkI GTs left the factory over the next few years.

Elsewhere road tests of the new five-bearing engine in the tourer found that, although it was a touch more refined at low revs, and despite an identical power output, it was a bit less free revving.

On the racetrack, success continued unabated. John Rhodes and Warren Banks won the two-day Brands Hatch 1,000-mile race in 8 DBL, while Paddy Hopkirk and Andrew Hedges achieved another second in class (11th overall) at Le Mans in DRX 255C.

For the 1966 12 Hours of Sebring, the company built an experimental 2,004cc, 150 brake-horsepower engine and used it in the Prototype class. Meanwhile the seemingly indefatigable GRX 307D took class wins at the Targa Florio (Timo Makinen/John Rhodes), Mugello (Andrew Hedges/Robin Widdows), Spa 1000-Kilometres (Andrew Hedges/Julien Vernaeve) and outright victory on the grueling, 84-hour Marathon de la Route (Hedges/Vernaeve).

1967: CHANGE IS AFOOT

Elsewhere in the BMC Empire (now technically called British Motor Holdings Ltd, after a merger with Jaguar), the Mini Cooper S—also prepared by the BMC Competition Department— stormed to success in the 1964, '66, and '67 editions of the Monte Carlo Rally. However, despite road versions of the Issigonis-designed icon selling in numbers only dreamt of by the MGB, all was not well. BMC had critically underpriced the car—something repeated with its Austin 1100 offshoot.

Change was once again the modus operandi over at MG in 1967, with the arrival of the MGB MkII. Focused on the US market, MG made this (and the new, six-cylinder MGC variant) its first model with an automatic gearbox. To achieve this, MG resized and reshaped the floorpan,

What a showstopper! The new MGB GT is announced in spectacular style at the Earls Court Motor Show in London, October 19, 1965.

now standardized with the GT's, and modified the body to accept the Borg-Warner Type 35 transmission mated to a 3.7:1 ratio rear axle. Ultimately this proved a dead end. With fewer than 4,000 sold, MG dropped it after six years. US buyers of British sporting wares, it seemed, wanted a stick shift.

The manual gearbox front changed to a much tougher, all-synchromesh four-speed unit (again shared with the MGC, but with an MGB-specific casing), while the GT's Salisbury rear axle was standardized.

Other changes included a new radiator, a pre-engaged starter motor, negative earth electrics, and two-speed (now plastic switched) window wipers.

In the cabin, the first tentative signs of what became a more than decade-long battle with North American Federal Safety (and later emissions) legislation made itself known. Concessions necessitated an energy-absorbing steering column, padded fascia and column stalk-operated lights, indicators and overdrive, as well as dual-circuit brakes for a swiftly changing US market.

The reception for the MkII (it only actually wore that designation in Australia) was instant—who wouldn't want a new and improved MGB? There was a resounding rebound effect as production of MkI Tourers, which had dipped from 22,675 in 1966 to 14,568 in 1967, rose to 17,247 MkII variants in 1968, leaving rivals in its wake on its way to an all-time high in 1972.

Despite the earlier arrival of the production GT, only one ever graced the racetrack as tourers almost always got the nod due to their lighter weight. Built for the 1967 season, LBL 591E was the exception. It achieved a class win for Paddy Hopkirk and Andrew Hedges at the 12 Hours of Serbing, before the MGB works vehicles ceded to the more specialized, next-generation MGC GTS models.

1968–1973

BMC's financial difficulties came home to roost in early 1968, forcing its hand and resulting in a May merger with Leyland Motor Corporation Limited. At the newly formed British Leyland Motor Corporation, MG found itself under the same banner as longtime arch nemesis Triumph.

Abingdon relied on annual cosmetic rejigging to keep the MGB fresh, adding Rostyle wheels, reclining seats, and a recessed grille (a strange affair with the MG badge in the center, with the hood retaining the surrounding badge bulge) in late 1969. That same year, cabin color choices were simplified to Henry Ford basics: you could

(Below) An arty period shot at Blenheim Palace in Woodstock, Oxfordshire, accentuates the stylish lines honed by the designers at Carrozzeria Pininfarina.

(Opposite) The arrival of the GT instantly endowed the MGB with a more practicality. Buyers could now say goodbye to wind-in-your-hair motoring and hello to an elegant and sporty grand tourer.

THE EX234

A proposed replacement for the MGB, the Pininfarina-designed 1967 EX234 prototype was a very Italian-looking thing. Unlike many prototypes, it survives to this day.

With a two-year gestation period for any new model, Abingdon's designers and engineers already had the post-MGB world in mind in 1967. After all, come 1969 the B would be in production for as long as the MGA. Little could those involved have imagined the upheavals of the coming decade.

Initially they considered upgrading the MGB to all-independent rear suspension, but cost once again blocked the path. Instead they designed the all-new car (codenamed EX234) for fitment of both the 1,275cc A-Series and 1,798cc B-Series engines. The plan was to replace both the MGB and, by keeping it light in weight, the smaller-engined Midget in a single stroke.

Engineers fitted a 1,275cc engine and hydrolastic suspension (by then de rigueur within the corporation) to a rolling chassis with a wheelbase 4 inches (10 cm) shorter the MGB's. Italian coachbuilder Pininfarina constructed a delicate-looking steel-and-alloy body that had definite shades

of both the Fiat 850 and Alfa's 105-Series Spiders, as well as Carrozzeria Frua's AC 428 Convertible, while still managing to resemble its actual predecessors.

Despite its sensual styling cues and shorter wheelbase, the biggest revelation was in the cabin, which clever packaging ensured was more spacious (even incorporating plus-two rear seats).

On its return to the UK, it was fitted with Lockheed disc brakes at Abingdon before being comprehensively tested. The general consensus for this fresh, futuristic car seems to have been that it was a fine one to drive, with even road manners.

However, by 1968 it had been abandoned. Multiple factors played a part, including committing considerable future development funds versus continuing with models then still flying out of the factory—and the looming costs of meeting ever-tightening North American safety and exhaust legislations for those very same cars.

have any color as long as it was black. And engineers paired the automatic gearbox with a 3.7:1-ratio rear axle to improve off-the-line acceleration.

A Leyland modernization drive in 1970 spawned yet more (minor) attempts to update the MGB. Vinyl replaced the leather seat facings and a new steering wheel with alloy spokes and faux leather rim took up residence. Two years later, a revised fascia with new color schemes and minor trim and fittings updates followed, and then an update to the grille replaced the unpopular 1969 style.

MGB production hit its high point in 1972, with just short of 40,000 cars (26,222 tourers and 13,171 GTs) leaving the factory. That the hardtop GT remained responsible for a third of all sales proved just what a versatile, do-everything (sports, touring, commuter, and family car) model it was.

However, 1973 saw it pulled from the US market, which had to make do with just the softtop. They removed the unsuccessful auto-box as an option in all markets.

1974–1978

Radial ply tires and overdrive were now standard on all MGBs, and new National Highway Traffic Safety Administration (NHTSA) regulations mandated large rubber block overriders—quickly nicknamed "Sabrinas," after the stage name of the well-endowed British model/actress Norma Ann Sykes—in 1974.

This was merely the prelude to a truly seismic facelift later that year. At the behest of the North American insurance industry, Federal impact laws now required

MkII MGB had a reshaped floorpan, which now allowed fitment of an optional Borg Warner automatic gearbox (manual, here). The steering column was now energy absorbing and the fascia padded.

(Left) This very of-the-period North American advertising shot shows the new front grille arrangement with badge in the center, which still left the original badge plinth in place.

(Opposite) Timo Makinen and John Rhodes's MGB Roadster GRX 307D engages in some handling shenanigans on the way to a class win on the 1966 Targa Florio in Sicily.

cars to have the ability to withstand a 5-miles-per-hour (8 km/h) impact with no resultant damage to essential lighting. New Marleyfoam Ltd, 5-miles-per-hour black polyurethane front and rear safety bumpers transformed the look (and more) of the MGB.

They were a neat solution and fitted fairly well— certainly compared to others, such as the Fiat 124 Spider's overhanging double chrome bar items—but their black appearance was incongruous, especially on lighter-colored bodywork. Painting them to match was out of the question, as the only solution involved using cyanide-based paint.

Engineers raised the chassis by 1.5 inches (3.81 cm) so the headlamps met new laws requiring them to be 16 to 20 inches (40.6 to 50.8 cm) above the ground. Under the skin there was considerable extra chassis metalwork that, when combined with the bumpers themselves, added just over 110 pounds (50 kg) in weight, and performance suffered as a result. Even worse, prior to release, testing revealed that it suffered severe roll-induced understeer

at the limit. Abingdon's solution was to delete the front anti-roll bar, endowing it with roll-on, roll-off ferry cornering characteristics. This made "…the car roll-oversteer too readily, and therefore somewhat twitchy even under public road conditions," said *Autocar* of the changes, in its April 1975 Auto Test. It wasn't until 1977 that MG found a suitable solution (and one that should have featured from the start): stiffened suspension, a rear anti-roll bar, and an uprated front anti-roll bar.

If UK buyers had to suffer the indignity of US-enforced changes, at least they didn't have to suffer the by-product of its new Federal emissions laws: a detuned single carburetor engine with a paltry 65 brake horsepower.

The onset of the first oil crisis and resultant recession, as well as internal organization strife, caused BLMC to collapse. Nationalization by Harold Wilson's government followed in 1975, with the company renamed Leyland Cars. That year also saw the arrival of gold badges (front bumper, steering wheel, and trunk lid/tail gate) to celebrate MG's "golden jubilee." In April they released the

Anniversary Edition, with 751 built (one was destroyed in a newspaper publicity stunt).

In 1977 a zip-out rear window arrived, as did Michael Edwardes as Chairman of the once again renamed British Leyland Cars. This heralded dark times ahead as Edwardes sought asset consolidation through factory closures. And Abingdon sat firmly in his sights.

1979-1980

In its last few years, the MGB soldiered on, as did the factory that produced it. March 1979 saw the arrival of a US-spec Limited Edition model, with black paint, side stripes, and cast alloy wheels.

Come the new decade, the modern metallic paints, alloy wheels, and contemporary cabin finishes could mask the MGB's age, but the suspension that had just passed muster when new and appeared outdated by 1970 was now positively antediluvian as 1980 approached.

"MGB. We complain. British Leyland makes money. Time stands still," was the title of a 1979 *Sports & GT* cars feature in the US. Yet still people bought them. The car's combination of reliability, simplicity, performance, looks, and, though anchored firmly in the sixties, its racing history remained relevant to the car itself.

Abingdon, earmarked for closure, released two final Limited Edition models. These UK LEs, of which 580 were built, were constructed and stored prior to the end of production, with the last MGB, a White Tourer for the Japanese market, rolling off the production line on Wednesday, October 22. Two days later Abingdon was no more. To think the small factory that Morris had bought in 1929 had risen from producing 50 cars a month to, at its height, 500 MGBs a week, with another 250 Sprites,

(Opposite top) The front profile looked better-resolved and certainly more pleasing than many rival manufacturers' efforts.

(Opposite bottom) While this rear bumper looks a touch cumbersome, it's a later example in which handling had at least been improved somewhat by the addition of front and rear anti-roll bars and stiffened suspension.

(Left) Post 1977 cars had a new fascia and an opening glove box. This example sports a relatively sober interior color (and aftermarket steering wheel), compared to some of the exceedingly seventies ones that were available.

Midgets, and Austin-Healeys built on sister production lines—it'd been one hell of a ride.

Over an 18-year period the MGB in all incarnations had sold over half a million units (it took Mazda's exquisite MX-5/Miata to better that). Even in its final year of production, it still sold well. It was the last MG sold in the US, which was criminal given the appetite, goodwill, and esteem in which it was held there.

If you were to sum up the MGB today in one word it would be *legend*, and, in a phrase, *the* quintessential British classic car.

The Limited Edition models signified the end of an era. However, more modern interior and exterior finishes couldn't mask the underpinnings' early-Sixties (and earlier) roots.

This Pewter Silver 1980 MGB GT Limited Edition came complete with eye-catching paint finish and five-spoke alloy wheels.

1962–1967
MGB

Models	Tourer (£690–£747), GT (£825–£865)	Gearbox	4-speed manual, optional overdrive from January 1963
Construction	Steel monocoque	Automatic	n/a
Length	153.3 in (389.4 cm)	Final Drive Ratio	3.91:1
Width	59.7 in (151.6 cm)	Steering	Rack and pinion
Height	Tourer, 49.4 in (125.5 cm), GT, 49.8 in (126.5 cm)	Front Suspension	Independent by coil springs, wishbones, and lever-arm dampers, anti-roll bar (optional on Tourer until chassis No. 108039)
Wheelbase	91 in (231.1 cm)		
Weight	Tourer, 2,031 lb (921 kg), GT, 2,190 lb (993.4 kg)	Rear Suspension	Live axle on half-elliptic leaf springs, lever-arm dampers
Engine Size	1,798cc	Tires	5.60 × 14 in
Engine Format	In-line 4-cylinder	Brakes	10.75 in (27.3 cm) disc brakes, front; 10 in (25.4 cm) drums, rear
Carburetion	2 × HS4 SU carburetors		
Max Bhp	95 bhp @ 5,400 rpm	0 to 60 mph	12.2 sec (Tourer), 13.6 sec (GT)
Max Torque	110 lb-ft @ 3,000 rpm	Top Speed	Tourer, 103 mph (166km/h); GT, 101 mph (162.5 km/h)
		Fuel Economy	26 mpg (US, 21.65 mpg)

1967–1974
As above for MGB Mk II, except

Models	Tourer (£770–£1,483), GT (£889–£1,504)	Max Torque	97 lb-ft @ 2,900 rpm
Weight	Tourer 2,140 lb (970.7 kg), GT 2,260 lb (1,025.1 kg)	Automatic	Optional
Max Bhp	82 bhp @ 5,400 rpm		

1975–1980
As above for post-1974 MGB, except

Models	Tourer (£1,579–£6,445), GT (£1,796–£6,937)	**Engine (US federal markets)**	
Weight	Tourer 2,253 lb (1,021.9 kg), GT 2,615 lb (1,186.1 kg)	Automatic	Optional
		Carburetion	Zenith-Stromberg carburetor
Length	166 in (421.6 cm)	Max Bhp	65 bhp @ 4,600 rpm
Height	50.25 in (127.6 cm)	Max Torque	92 lb-ft @ 2,500 rpm
Engine (UK market)		0 to 60 mph	Tourer 18.3 sec (GT withdrawn in federal markets)
Max Bhp	84 bhp @ 5,250 rpm		
Max Torque	104 lb-ft @ 2,500 rpm	Top Speed	Tourer, 90 mph (144.8 km/h)

CHAPTER 10

C FOLLOWS B

The concept behind a larger-engined MGB was sound, but its execution proved troublesome. Despite a somewhat convoluted design process that included a lack of development time and money, and a somewhat underwhelming press reaction, the MGC was a decent GT car. And via their racing exploits, the wild purpose-built GTS variants would achieve legendary status.

The "new" six-cylinder engine was, in fact, a rushed, cost-restricted development of the Austin-Healey 3000's existing 3-liter unit.

The two commissioned projects (ADO 51 and ADO 52) used the MGB, which was swallowing considerable development funds, as their basis. As before, differences between the two marques' cars were to be skin deep, both with the same six-cylinder engine. The question was, which one?

The existing BMC C-Series unit was too large and heavy, as it severely compromised underpinnings designed for the significantly lighter four-cylinder unit. After discounting an Australian six-cylinder version of the B-Series (which utilized triple carburetors) because of cost and logistical considerations, the BMC Engines Branch Factory at Coventry got the task of developing a suitable power plant.

The engine also powered the upcoming Austin 3.0-liter sedan. But when engineering team lead Enever proposed a more compact, short-stroke design for the sports cars, he was overruled. From a design perspective, the eventual result was little different (save for a seven- rather than four-main-bearing crankshaft) than the originally discarded C-Series unit, was disappointing in the extreme, and directly reflected MG's loss of project control within its cumbersome parent company.

With the saga of an unsatisfactory engine unfolding, Donald Healey pulled the plug on the Austin-Healey ADO 51 project and embarked on what became the eventual dead end of updating the 3000 with a 4.0-liter Princess R Rolls-Royce engine (canceled after building only one prototype and two preproduction Austin-Healey 4000s).

Back in the MG camp, instead of the promised significantly lighter, smaller, and more powerful engine, the company had to make do with one that, at 567 pounds (257 kg), was just 20 pounds (9.1 kg) lighter than the old C-Series unit and a staggering 209 pounds (95 kg) heavier than the four-cylinder B-Series MGBs. It also produced 5 brake horsepower less than the Austin-Healey 3000 on which it was based. The engineering team was able to shoehorn it into the engine bay, but only after serious modifications.

The donor car's crossmember was also too substantial and had to be replaced by a thinner, U-shaped item—with incorporated suspension top and engine mounts—that wouldn't foul the new engine's sump. Both this and the vastly increased weight of the power unit necessitated a complete front suspension redesign. Out went the B's coil springs, lever-arm dampers, and lower wishbones, replaced by stronger longitudinal torsion bars, telescopic dampers, and front anti-roll bar setup. At the rear the B's hydraulic lever-arm damper and half leaf-spring setup remained. New inner fenders, remodeled floor pressings, and a new alloy hood (with a large bump to clear both an engine and radiator sitting farther forward, and a smaller, teardrop-shaped bump for the front SU carburetor) completed the rework.

To cope with a 50 percent power increase, engineers fitted a stronger, all-synchromesh four-speed gearbox (with optional overdrive), although, in a first for MG, a Borg Warner 35 three-speed automatic unit was also offered. Both were shared with the MkII MGB.

Anticipating a heavier nose, the team added a lower-geared steering rack and reduced castor angle. Larger Girling front disc brakes and a longer-legged Salisbury rear axle completed the mechanical setup.

Unfortunately, when it came to aesthetics, the development pot was most definitely empty, so the only adaptations were larger, 15-inch (38.1 cm) wheels, that multihumped hood, and the replacement of C for B on the rear chrome script—small potatoes indeed.

1967

In 1966 BMC competition manager Turner decided to build a series of racing cars based on the upcoming MGC to contest in the sports car prototype category. Superficially the lightweight MGC GTS resembled the production car, but underneath the skin each was highly modified.

The company constructed six bodies using MGC pressed-steel chassis sections as their bases but fitting them with a range of alloy panels, including doors,

fenders, roof, hood, trunk, and valances. To fit racing tires and wheels, the wheel arches were highly flared.

There was a problem, though. Due to a delay delivering engines, the first racing example MBL 546E (immediately christened Mabel) was ready prior to the roadgoing MGC's big press reveal. With secrecy firmly in mind, BMC made the decision to eschew the six-cylinder engine and instead endow Mabel with a bored-out, 2,004cc four-cylinder MGB unit. The good news was that the new car's visual similarity to its sibling meant that, combined with the power plant, for all intents and purposes to onlookers the racer was simply a highly fettled B.

Entered in the 1967 Targa Florio, this 150-brake-horse-power racing mutt acquitted itself reasonably well at the hands of Paddy Hopkirk and Timo Mäkinen. Despite finishing down the field, it took third in class.

The road car finally arrived in October, with its launch at the Earls Court Motor Show. To onlookers, journalists, and public alike, it was immediately clear just how visually

(Above and opposite top)
Accommodating the radiator and front SU carburetor required additional hood bulges in the MGC.

(Opposite bottom) The interior was identical to the MGB's, save for a leather cover on the steering wheel rim.

(Above) Rub your eyes and look again, it's not a B but a C. Marginally higher ride height, hood bulges, and larger 15-in wheels are the telltale signs.

(Right) The use of the word "Sports" in marketing the MGC proved to be a considerable sticking point for those expecting the MGB's surefooted handling.

(Opposite) While imagery in a US advertisement hinted at the C being the perfect chariot for an illicit liaison, the caption emphasized familiar looks but a "new" car under the skin. But its visual similarity to the B helped seal its fate in period.

Much more than meets the eye

the new 6 cylinder

MGC
SPORTS AND G.T.

similar it was to its smaller-engine sibling. Even the interior was identical, save for a leather cover on the steering wheel rim. The serious increase in performance should have taken precedence, but already there were grumblings about the lack of extras on this new, more expensive model.

However, even before its presentation to the world's motoring press for testing, the tone for the MGC's reception had been set. In previous years, and with prior models, BMC's publicity department gained a reputation for being haphazard at best and downright defensive at worst. Therefore an element of the British motoring press was predisposed to being unhappy about the new car even before its arrival, and, as expected, a somewhat muddled launch followed. Having fought the enemy within on the engine front, MG found itself in familiar, frustrating territory.

While this no doubt didn't help, they weren't to blame for the car's underlying shortcomings, which journalists were quick to identify: the engine's turgid low-down nature and the effects of the car's nose-heavy character on steering and cornering.

The former may have been acceptable on an executive sedan, but for one with sporting pretensions it was anathema. The MGC rode beautifully and drove like a consummate grand tourer, but these aspects were lost as many took umbrage at MG continuing to insist on describing it as a sports car.

From the first test corner it was clear that the MGB's feline poise had been lost, replaced by more ponderous tendencies. In truth, although the new car's weight distribution had shifted forward (55.7/44.3 versus 52.6/47.4), a 14 percent higher center of gravity had the biggest effect, making it somewhat recalcitrant when faced with swift directional changes.

Contrary to public perception, not all initial reviews were negative. Writing in the December 1967 issue of *Autosport*, John Bolster praised the engine's "first impression of phenomenal smoothness," although he acknowledged the redesign resulted in it being down

on power. He also found the brakes "excellent" and that, overall, the MGC had "a long stride for covering many miles, or kilometres, in a day."

1968

Performance figures were reasonably good. Here was a genuine 120-mile-per-hour car that covered the 0-to-60 sprint in 10 seconds. However, the numbers could have been even better had the MGC's extra heft not negated most of the power increase and endowed it with a surfeit of understeer. In automatic form—with even more weight and fewer horses—matters were worse, as it was slower than a B from 0 to 60 (10.9 seconds).

Pricing was relatively competitive at £895 for the two-seater open-top tourer and £1,015 for the coupe (both excluding purchase tax). The automatic gearbox set you back £98 6s 3d, and the optional overdrive £61 9s 2d.

SEBRING SUCCESS

Her driver thoroughly tested "Mabel"—now endowed with the proper six-cylinder MGC engine—at Thruxton racetrack in 1968.

Race it on a Sunday, celebrate it on a Monday! The 1968 12 Hours of Sebring was a resounding success. The Midget, MGC, and Austin-Healey Sprite all finished first in class, and BMC ensured that everyone knew it.

Come 1968, with Peter Browning now at the competition department helm and the eventual showroom arrival of the MGC, the GTS could finally be endowed with a 202 brake horsepower racing version of the six-cylinder engine.

That year's 12 Hours of Sebring race proved a success. Paddy Hopkirk and Andrew Hedges piloted the C to tenth place overall, third in the Prototype Category, and first in the 2,500–3,000cc Prototype Class—MG's best ever placing at the track.

This went some way towards putting to bed the 1966 fate of MGB Roadster 8 DBL, which had thrown a connecting rod with just ninety minutes remaining when leading the Prototype Class.

Keen to celebrate category and class victories (the MG Midget came first overall in the 1,150–1,300cc Sports Car class, and the Austin-Healey Sprite took first in the 1,150–1,300cc Prototype class) in its key North American market, the company took out advertisements stating, "When BMC go on an Export Drive—the competition knows it!"

Later that year "Mabel" performed well again overseas on the Marathon de la Route at Germany's Nürburgring, coming in with a sixth-place finish overall driven by Julian Vernaeve, Andrew Hedges, and Tony Fall. This time a sister car, the experimental alloy-block-engined RMO 699F, accompanied it. Driven by Roger Enever (Syd Enever's son), Alec Poole, and Clive Baker, it retired from the 84-hour endurance event due to cooling issues.

If initial press receptions were frosty, it got a damned sight colder in the new year. In its August 1968 issue, *Car* magazine said it had driven "a supposed sports car totally devoid of sporting characteristics. Never mind, the Americans will buy it . . . because it looks right and it's an MG: serve them right!"

The first sentiment nicely summed up the general press consensus, although the second somewhat snide dig at North American cousins was a little unnecessary. In its March 1968 preview test, stateside magazine *Car and Driver* had already stated, "it's simply an evolutionary model—one that points out the danger of inbreeding."

Export market cars for North America differed in several ways. The braking system was dual-circuit instead of single and featured twin servos for increased stopping power. The padded dashboard had safer rubber switches. Carburetors were sealed in order to return unburned fuel to the engine, and the body received the side-marker lights and reflectors.

MGC production reached its height in 1968, with 2,566 tourers and 2,462 GT models constructed for all markets.

1969

The C's updated cabin now offered reclining seats for a modicum more comfort. To perk up performance, engineers rejigged gearbox and rear-axle ratios for the 1969 models by replacing the original 3.07:1 with a 3.31:1 unit in nonoverdrive form and, in overdrive form, changing the 3.31:1 to a 3.7:1 ratio. Automatics remained at 3.307:1.

The rest of the mechanical specification remained the same, which was a shame for an engine crying out for further developmental work. British Leyland subsumed BMC a few weeks into MGC production in 1967, and the reality was that, in its new world order, the products of the old British Motor Corporation sat far down the food chain.

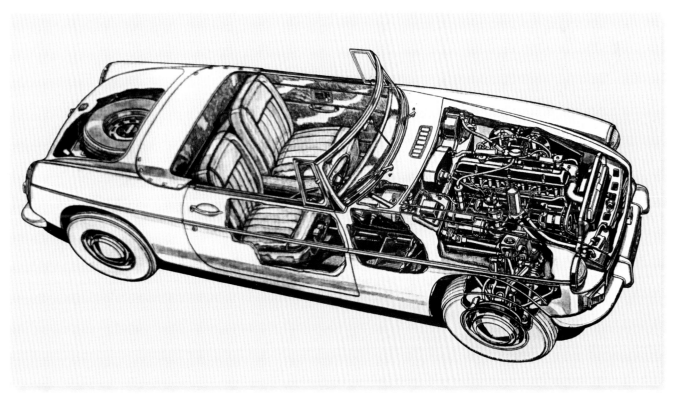

This cutaway drawing shows the added length of the six-cylinder engine. Note the radiator is now mounted right at the extremity of the nose.

THE UMS CARS—
A SPECIAL KIND OF C

As a post note, London MG agent University Motors bulk-bought the remaining unsold examples (believed to be in the order of 141 to 156 cars) and went on to charge buyers a sliding premium based on specification ordered. Some were fitted with Downton Engineering Works–tuned engines, which could be ordered in Stage 2 or 3 guises to improve power, torque, and economy.

After development of Mini engines had brought it recognition, Daniel Richmond's concern became BMC's official tuner in the early 1960s. From that point, almost all of the industrial giant's Works racers had been Downton-tuned—perhaps its greatest successes being the giant-killing Mini Cooper and Mini Cooper S rally cars.

Unlike with previous models, a Special Tuning booklet was never produced for the MGC. However, a Stage 1 cylinder-head kit—polished with new valves and springs and a matched inlet manifold—was approved by, marketed by, and available only through Abingdon's Special Tuning division.

However, if you wanted something a bit zestier, a visit to Downton Engineering Works was in order. There you could order a Stage 2 (No. 43) setup that added a 9.5:1 engine compression ratio, two three-branch exhaust manifolds, and a new dual-exhaust system for a 149-bhp net output at 5,500 rpm. It was capable of 0 to 60 miles per hour in 8.2 seconds and a 130-miles-per-hour top speed.

(Left) *A discreet Downton badge at the rear is the only indicator of tuning work.*

(Below) *The blue, red, and silver UMS badge, as fitted to Specials.*

(Opposite) *UM Specials had a modified grille with horizontal black slats and tended to have vinyl roofs, sunroofs, and painted hood bulges, as well as other random bodywork modifications. No two cars are identical, and this example sports a unique Cibie headlight arrangement.*

If that still wasn't enough, there was the feisty Stage 3 (No. 45) triple-carb conversion to the standard car's twin setup that brought in a new mixture control and progressive throttle assembly and three special inlet manifolds, as well as that extra carburetor. Its 174 bhp net at 5,500 rpm was good for 0 to 60 miles per hour in 7.3 seconds and a 130-miles-per-hour-plus top speed. *Autosport* had tested a Stage 2 car in November 1968 and found that its "improved flexibility and torque are valuable." It was a no-brainer that the very end-of-the-line University Motors Specials would continue to offer the Downton Engineering Works tuning options, although it's generally thought that only 11 UMS cars were converted.

Custom Car tested a Stage 2 UMS car in June 1970 and concluded that it was "a car for the serious performance enthusiast who needs bags of poke for long mileages." However, it continued "the whole handling was a lot better than we had been led to expect from earlier reports of the standard 'C'."

If the UMS Downton–tuned cars provided the model's zenith, it was clear that just one year after MGC production ended, perceptions of this much misunderstood model were already starting to change.

The substitution of one letter of the alphabet for another is the only difference to the rear of both GT and Tourer.

Unfortunately the changes for 1969 were lost on most. Mindsets most definitely had been firmly fixed. *Car and Driver* eventually delivered its final opinion in June 1969, calling the 1969 MGC "a totally bland motor-car" and measuring just a 0.1-second reduction in the 0 to 60 time compared to its earlier preview example.

The MGC's moment was drawing to a close. By September 1969, production ceased. In two years, they had constructed just 8,999 examples: 4,542 tourers and 4,457 GTs. Of these, 4,256 found their way to the US and 3,437 remained in the UK.

On the track, both racing MGC GTS cars returned to Sebring for what would be their last works outing but met with no real success. As with the production car, support for the last-ever BMC Competition Department–prepared race cars was at best half-hearted.

American customers subsequently purchased both racers. Bristol-based dealer and racing driver John Chatham bought the remaining bodyshells (later built as complete cars) and spare MGC GTS stock.

Ultimately developmental compromises, inept marketing, and lack of investment (both monetary and intellectual) hampered the standard car. Among all the "noise," perhaps journalist John Bolster was correct in his opinion: "It's unreasonable to treat a sports touring car as a sports racing car." Today's C owners would no doubt agree.

The source of much consternation as shown here in standard form, but in Downton Stage 3 form the six-cylinder unit could be tuned to produce up to 200 bhp.

1967–1968
MGC and MGC GT

Models	Tourer (£895), Coupe (£1,015)		Gearbox	4-speed manual (optional Laycock LH overdrive)
Construction	Steel monocoque		Automatic	Borg Warner Type 35
Length	153.2 in (389.1 cm)		Final Drive Ratio	3.91:1
Width	60 in (152.4 cm)		Steering	Rack and pinion
Height	Roadster, 50.25 in (127.6 cm); Coupe, 51.0 in (129.5 cm)		Front Suspension	Independent by unequal-length parallel wishbones and adjustable torsion bars, Armstrong telescopic dampers, antiroll bar
Wheelbase	91 in (231.1 cm)		Rear Suspension	Live axle on half-elliptic leaf springs, hydraulic lever-arm dampers
Weight	2,460 lb (1,116 kg), Coupe 2,610 lb (1,184 kg)			
Engine Size	2,912cc		Tires	165 HR 15 radial
Engine Format	In-line 6-cylinder		Brakes	Girling brakes—front 11.06 in (28.1 cm) discs; rear 9 in (22.9 cm) drums, vacuum servo assistance
Carburetion	2 × 1.75 SU HS6			
Max Bhp	145 @ 5,250 rpm		0 to 60 mph	9.8 sec
Max Torque	170 lb-ft @ 3,400 rpm		Top Speed	126 mph (202.77 km/h)
			Fuel Economy	19.3 mpg (US, 16.1 mpg)

1969
As above for 1969 model, except

Models	Tourer (£1,337), Coupe (£1,481)
Final Drive Ratio	Manual, 3.307:1 (overdrive, 3.7:1); automatic, 3.307:1
Top Speed	120 mph (193.1 km/h)

CHAPTER 11

V8!:
A NEW HIGH-PERFORMANCE MODEL

Despite the demise of the six-cylinder MGC, dreams of a high-performance MGB continued at Abingdon. It took the efforts, and outstanding results, of a talented individual to spur MG's parent company to action. This time the development and production processes were significantly easier, and the performance results markedly more impressive. The new high-performance MGB GT V8 was most rapid car ever to leave Abingdon.

As this 1967 MGB Roadster (endowed with a small-block Ford 289 engine), and numerous repeated journalistic pleadings, demonstrated, there was more-than-adequate US appetite for a V8 car.

"We can think of no reason why BLMC are not producing it themselves, and their product planners ought to be ashamed at not having spotted this potential market," said *Autocar* on May 25, 1972. The prompt for this withering putdown was, of course, its auto test of the low-volume Costello MGB GT V8.

Kent-based independent engineer Ken Costello had been shoehorning the small-block Rover V8 engine into a variety of MGB Roadsters and GTs since 1970, with much success.

In 1969 he established the concept's feasibility by fitting a red MGB Roadster with an Oldsmobile 215 engine (the Rover unit's precursor) and achieved impressive performance levels. Based on his second attempt, a 1970 MGB GT, *Autocar*'s test car featured his now-proven mechanical specification of the all-alloy Rover V8 (in 150-brake-horsepower form) mated to a standard MGB gearbox, larger 9.5-inch (24.1 cm) clutch, and a 3.07:1 ratio rear axle. Suspension, braking (save for harder front

pads), and steering systems remained unchanged from MGB specifications, and visually the car was identifiable by the black alloy "egg-box" grille, a V8 Costello badge on its rump, and a fiberglass hood with large power hump (to clear the carburetors).

Unlike the MGC, fitment of the Rover V8 actually resulted in a lighter car and had the additional benefit of shifting weight distribution from the MGB's 52.6:47.4 to the sports car's holy grail of 50:50. The testers noted its surefootedness, wet-road traction, and a lack of axle tramp, but their primary focus was the sheer level of clout available. Its 58-percent brake horsepower and 82-percent torque increases over the standard B-Series unit saw the Costello car hit 0 to 60 miles per hour in just 7.8sec—a whopping 5.2 seconds quicker than a standard MGB GT.

The only negatives were, in the main, noted as being of a British Leyland, rather than a Costello, ilk (i.e., factors intrinsic to the factory-produced donor vehicle): a poor level of cabin equipment, low-set seats, and a high level of wind noise. The one that wasn't BLMC's fault was price. At £2,443.24—rising to £2,616.31 with extras such as overdrive, radial tires, alloy wheels, and a heated backlight fitted—accessing that V8 performance came at a significant cost.

Despite this, in summation, *Autocar* praised the "very professional standard of the finish," and stated, "as a conversion, we rate this car as perfect and as a model in its own right it deserves the highest praise."

Did the British Leyland Motor Company deserve the journal's scorn? Well, by the time of the feature's 1972 publication, development of BLMC's own in-house model was in fact already well underway. It's almost certain the magazine knew this, and the sharp, scolding tone of its message smacked more of indulgement in an overt case of BMLC-bashing rather than a pointed call to action.

Despite the MGC's fate, as far back as the late sixties Abingdon's engineers continued to harbor thoughts of a high-performance MGB. British Motor Holdings's spring 1968 merger with the Leyland Motor Company suddenly brought the Rover V8 into play. However, in a 1970 internal memo to Lord Stokes, chief engineer Charles Griffin stated that in order to fit one in an MGB, "the car would have to be widened at least three and a half inches, so obviously this is not feasible."

Griffin's memo was perhaps a quickly written, stock management response, and he likely was unaware that Australian magazine *Sports Car World* had, three years earlier in its November 1967 issue, reported on the fitment of an alloy Buick V-8 in an MGB. The key points being that this had been achieved "with no body mods and a single exhaust outlet."

One thing's for sure: both the Abingdon team and MG enthusiasts *were* acutely aware. The idea of a V-8–engined MGB caused considerable excitement, and serious thought was immediately given as to how this could be carried out. Unfortunately Abingdon did not have the budget, nor could it gain the BLMC senior management team's approval.

Their frustration was further increased by the arrival (during the same year as Griffin's memo) of Costello's car and, with it quickly gaining an ever-burgeoning reputation in the motoring press, BLMC soon had no option but to take an interest.

Invited to submit a car for assessment, on arrival at Longbridge, Costello (who hadn't made an appointment, he simply turned up) was whisked off for lunch while others at the company gave his vehicle a thorough appraisal. It obviously left a positive impression, as he was soon on his way to the company's Berkeley Square London HQ, where it was Lord Stokes's turn to see what on Earth all the fuss was about. Similarly impressed by the conversion's sheer gusto (he must surely have questioned his subordinate's earlier advice on viability), Stokes commissioned Costello to produce a car for MG that would later be assessed in detail by a team including Don Hayter. The parties also entered into negotiations for Austin-Morris Engineering's approval of Costello's

conversions and a supply of engines and rear axles direct from the British Leyland distribution network.

Unencumbered by the issues that came with being a consituent part of a large and relatively inflexible commercial group (budgetary constraints, labor relations, and managerial politics to name a few), Costello had been able to stride forward and put his impressive conversion into production.

When BLMC saw just how successful a V-8–engined MGB could be, the sterling, professional efforts of this Kent-based artisan engineer finally provoked the industrial giant into action.

1973: MINOR CHANGES, MAJOR GO

Given the go-ahead, Abingdon's engineers had the prototype ADO 75 up and running within an astonishing four weeks, and the preproduction prototypes well before December 1972, but the production vehicle itself wouldn't arrive for another two years until its August 1973 launch

After considerable to and fro, the board decided to build the new model in manual coupe form only and, even more surprisingly, restricted to the UK market.

At a ticket price of £2,293.96, it significantly under-cut the Costello machine and had an instant impact on his order book. Just to be sure though, Lord Stokes turned off the engine supply taps—a harsh but sensible business decision.

The new MGB GT V8 was certainly a mouthful to pronounce, but its development had been a far simpler undertaking than that of the MGC. This time there was no need for a comprehensive reworking of the front end. The V-8 (here in low compression 8.25:1, 137 brake horsepower Range Rover form) slotted straight in with just a modicum of necessary engine bay panel reshaping.

(Below) At last, the factory V-8 effort arrives. Promotional ads were few and far between, but this one emphasizes the minimal visual differences (grille-mounted badge and alloy wheels) between the new car and existing four-cylinder MGB GT.

(Opposite) This Costello V8 engine bay shows the power plant still in standard Rover form. A custom fiberglass hood with a large power hump was needed to clear the top-mounted carburetors.

The new MGB GT V8

THE MGB WITH THE V8 ENGINE HAS LAYCOCK OVERDRIVE, BRAKE SERVO, ALLOY WHEELS, TWIN ELECTRIC COOLING FANS, TINTED WINDOWS AND HEAD RESTRAINTS AS STANDARD EQUIPMENT

THE "ROVER" V8

Or, that should be the General Motors 215-cubic-inch V-8. Originally developed for the North American compact sedan market, the all-alloy engine powered about 750,000 Buick Specials (including the Skylark), Oldsmobile F-85s, and Pontiac Tempests before changing market demographics and reduced iron-block engine production costs saw it become surplus to requirements after just three years.

In 1964, during a business development trip, Rover managing director William Martin-Hurst spotted one on a workshop floor of Fond du Lac, Wisconsin–based specialist Mercury Marine, and the rest as they say, is history.

Shipped to the UK and fitted to a Rover 2000 test-bed its performance knocked the company's chairman Spencer Wilks's proverbial socks off—highlighting in an instant its possibilities as an alternative to Rover's then aging, and somewhat anemic, four-cylinder units.

With the rights secured, its engineers turned to "Rover-izng" it, with production shifting from the US die-cast to the British sand-cast method (negating the coolant-related reliability issues of the original); this involved the incorporation of pressed-fit cylinder liners, with UK-sourced ancillaries (including twin SU carburettors) replacing American units.

Simple, lightweight, and with first-class fuel economy, fitted to the Rover P5B, P6, and Land (and later, Range) Rover, the V-8 proved to be a performance revelation. However, it's both the unit's longevity and reliability, coupled with its sheer range of applications, that have proven the essential value of the original design. From the 161 brake horsepower original through its first sports car deployment in the Morgan Plus 8, to Rover SD1 3500, Triumph TR8, and Ginetta G33—to name but a few—

Neat reworking of the twin carburetor arrangement, including the use of an innovative "lobster claw" air cleaner design, made a hood bulge unnecessary.

on to its monstrous 5.0-liter 340 brake horsepower form in the 1994 TVR Chimaera, for over fifty years the Rover V8, that quintessential Anglicized American engine, powered a huge number of sedan, coupe, 4×4, sport, race, and military vehicles.

(Opposite) A lack of visual differentiation from the standard MGB disappointed many, but it proved a decidedly deceptive sleeper capable of surprising many higher cachet machines—even more so here, without the production car's identifying tailgate-mounted V8 badge.

Dunlop cast-alloy wheels are a signature V8 styling indicator (later shared with 1975 Jubilee GTs).

No doubt still wary of the criticism of its predecessor's necessary hood humps, it featured a bespoke inlet manifold arrangement that moved the twin SU carburetors towards the rear of the engine and lower down, allowing fitment of a standard MGB item. Its "lobster claw" intake shrouds featured thermostatically controlled bimetal valves, which drew warm air in from around the engine when cold and cool air when it was warm, allowing it to meet new European ECE15 pollution standards. MG altered the steering rack position and added twin electric fans to ensure the big 3.5-liter engine kept a cool head.

Unlike Costello, MG's engineers decided to adapt the gearbox, suspension, and braking systems. This was no doubt another sensible decision, since Abingdon's car was a series production vehicle rather than a "hot" aftermarket conversion, and, perhaps even more so, because many in the development team felt that power and torque outputs (the latter a lofty 193 pound feet at 2,900 rpm) placed the car particularly close to the original design's limits.

Although the gearbox was the same basic MGB four-speed manual unit, the MG team revised the ratios and switched to the Salisbury axle in 3.07:1 form with Laycock overdrive now as standard. The suspension—ahead of the curve when new in 1962 but by now showing its age—benefitted from stiffer springs (police specification at the rear), while the brakes were now the standard servo assisted, with thicker front discs.

The team at MG completed all these mechanical developments on the thinnest of development budgets, and that applied doubly so to cosmetic changes. Cabin modifications were negligible, while the exterior benefitted from the addition of "V8" badges (all filched from Rover) on the front grille, the rump, and the nearside front fender; a British Leyland badge also appeared on the latter. From a distance, smart-looking (and extremely

This interior remains pure MGB, but four-cylinder car optional extras, such as seat head restraints, Sundym tinted windows, and a heated rear window, were now standard fitment.

(Above and opposite) Unlike the later MG effort, the privateer offered both GT and Roadster options. Note the engorged hood and deep-lip spoiler sitting below its egg-crate grille.

An oversized "V" and smaller remaining badge script indicates something special under the hood, but buyers paid a considerable premium for V8 power.

strong) new Dunlop D4 14-inch (36 cm) wheels, with a cast alloy center and steel rims, provided the only identifier of the car as a new model in its own right.

MG threw in optional extras—including the overdrive, Sundym tinted windows, a heated rear window, seat head restraints, and twin door mirrors—as standard fitment. Despite this, and also significantly undercutting the Costello car, the question of cost, and value for money, once again proved crucial.

At launch, accessing the MGC's superior performance cost buyers a 14 percent premium (£1,094 versus £1,249) over an MGB. Come 1973 and for the MGB GT V8, that rose dramatically to 48 percent (£1,547 versus £2,294). Abingdon's engineers would have no doubt quite happily thrown caution to the wind and further developed the model, but once again its overseers had financially tied their hands limiting what they could do.

The press reviews were mixed. There was no question that the performance was in a different league from the standard four-cylinder car and, despite on paper having a lower power output than the MGC, its torque-laden nature of delivery put that model to shame.

"What the bald figures cannot convey is the utter smoothness, refinement and lack of drama with which the unit performs, and the delightful surge when accelerating hard . . ." said *Autosport* in its August 16, 1973, road test.

Other plaudits lauded the driveline and the effortless, long performance legs (28.5 miles per hour per 1,000 rpm) with which it endowed the car; its handling—unlike the MGC, little changed from that of the nimble-footed four-cylinder MGB; and that the fuel consumption return was impressive for such a large engine. With a 0 to 60-miles-per-hour time of 8.6 seconds (*Motor*)

A QUESTION OF AMERICA

If pricing had a detrimental effect on the MGB GT V8 in the UK (it could, and should, have been lower), then the decision to withhold the model from MG's largest market beggars belief.

Almost 80 percent of the marque's output found homes overseas, with the vast majority going to the USA. Factor in that around two-thirds of those were of the soft-top variety (even in the dreary-skied UK, the Mk1 MGB tourer had outsold its hardtop sibling by a ratio of 2.42:1), and that secondary choice to limit it to GT-only form looked foolhardy.

At the September 28, 1971, meeting of BLMC's Product Policy Group, its chairman, George Turnbull, stated that, "the Austin-Morris would only proceed with the project providing it met future legal requirements for the USA."

Don Hayter, speaking to the MG Car Club's V8 Register, later recalled that "the V8 was clear to go to America—it had crash tested and emission tested and was ready to go if the management said OK." However, by 1972, after much indecision, while the 1800 MGB and MGB GT were cleared for export to the US, the group had reversed this viewpoint and abandoned the idea of a North American release.

There's no doubt, as continuing healthy MGB sales demonstrated (19,546 tourers and 10,208 GTs, in 1973), US appetite for the marque remained strong, and the home of the V-8 engine would surely have welcomed the model with open arms.

Certainly, in an article titled "MG V-8, There's good news and bad news"—the good: fitment of the V8; the bad: no US release—in the October 1973 issue of *Motor* magazine International, John Blunsden felt it to be an error, opining, ". . . roll on the day when they can make enough of a replacement model to satisfy all demands, not least that from the country which for so many years has provided MG with its best export market."

More so as, in the same feature, he praised the fact that "the MGB's 'chuckability' through smoother-surfaced corners remains unimpaired," and that, despite its "relatively effortless cruising potential, the car is in its most enjoyable environment on twisty roads where the middle-range torque and responsive handling characteristics can be used to their full advantage."

The effects on MG of the internecine politics at play and resultant decisions made, by both the Product Policy Group and other upper echelons of BLMC management, were surely the institutional equivalent of having someone blindfold you, tie your hands behind your back, and then shoot you in the foot. The Rover V8 eventually reached North America in 1987, via the Range Rover—it's just a pity no one connected the dots some 15 years earlier.

Of course, over the last few decades—shorn of production date, capacities, and target market considerations—the V8 has subsequently come to be viewed as something of an undiscovered sports car. GT cars, by their very nature, tend to forego sporting characteristics in the pursuit of kilometer-devouring abilities—with the MGB GT V8, you get both.

Owners of one can luxuriate in the knowledge that they own a rare, rapid, and very capable sporting coupe.

(Opposite) Despite not being an export model, in the interests of rationalization the V8 also gained the "rubber bumper" treatment.

would report just 7.7 seconds in its August 1973 issue) and a 125-miles-per-hour top speed, it was the most rapid product ever to come out of Abingdon. In addition, it was a consummate grand tourer capable of effortlessly devouring large distances.

On the negative side were wind noise, poor low-speed ride quality, and somewhat harsh suspension. The sheer refinement of the Rover V8 drew attention to a barrage of wind noise at speed that had hitherto been masked by four-cylinder unit's aural exertions.

However, the question of price had the biggest effect, as the ghost of MGC past came to call. Despite being severely criticized for a lack of distinction from its smaller-engined sibling, the MGB GT V8 continued in an almost identical manner. Its lack of visual exterior and cabin differentiation wasn't well received. "Too expensive," cried *Autosport*; while *Motor Sport* perhaps hit the nail on the head saying, "Had the new wine been put into the old bottle a few years ago and a programme of continuous development maintained, then MG could have had themselves a world-beater." As it was, high-performance thrills could be had significantly cheaper with, for instance, the £1,824 Ford Capri 3000GLX, and, thrust into a price bracket with significantly higher-specified rivals—including the likes of the Datsun 240Z and Reliant Scimitar GTE—it was difficult to argue with those critics' opinions of its ticket price.

Then, on October 6, Egypt and Syria attacked Israel, starting the Yom Kippur war, which in turn drew in the US and Soviet Union superpowers. In response to the former establishing an emergency supply line to Israel, the OPEC oil-producing nations doubled, and then doubled again, the price of oil. Its effects weren't felt immediately, but they were certainly felt.

By the end of the year, the company had produced 1,070 MGB GT V8s, but that would be a production high.

The Thames Valley Constabulary ordered three V8s, fitted them with Police accoutrements, and ran them as unmarked "Q-cars."

1974: ARRIVAL OF THE "RUBBER BUMPERS"

There was no reflective glory from a high-powered and bubble-arched, successful race car, which was a shame as the Rover V8's effortless high-speed performance, low-stressed nature, and superb reliability would have almost certainly lent itself well to long-distance events, such as Sebring and Le Mans.

Instead, as fuel prices rose and the decade descended ever further into a combined political and economic maelstrom, public perception of large-engined cars as thirsty great devils hit hard on the sales front—despite the fact that with an average fuel consumption of 25 miles per gallon it was only 3 miles per gallon less efficient than the four-cylinder GT.

An enforced change towards the end of the year didn't help matters. Despite the model's home market-only status, the so-called "1974½ facelift" saw the entire MGB range (V8 included) endowed with the new Marley foam 5-miles-per-hour black polyurethane safety bumpers.

1975–1976:
THE END IS NIGH

Changes for 1975 were minor in the extreme, limited to some very small tweaks to trim items. To celebrate the marque's "Golden Jubilee," all chrome MG badges gained a gold finish, with their background changed from red to black, while the rear B GT badge's metallic blue lettering was now also black. Just one MGB GT V8 Jubilee Special (with its British Racing Green paint and black-and-gold V8-style alloys, as per the MGB variants) was also produced.

The following year, a "GT" flash badge appeared at the top of the C-pillar, disguising a previously lead-loaded join. However, by August of 1976 MGB sales literature no longer carried the V8 as an option.

The end, when it came the following month, saw one of the most accomplished performing MGs ever produced cease production. BLMC had produced just 183 cars in that final calendar year, and 2,591 in total.

1973–1974
MGB GT V8

Models	Coupe (£1,925)	Gearbox	4-speed manual with Laycock LH overdrive
Construction	Steel monocoque	Automatic	n/a
Length	154.7 in (392.9 cm)	Final Drive Ratio	3.07:1
Width	60 in (152.4 cm)	Steering	Rack and pinion
Height	50 in (127 cm)	Front Suspension	Independent wishbones, coil springs, lever-arm dampers, and anti-roll bar
Wheelbase	91 in (231.1 cm)		
Weight	2,387 lb (1,082.7 kg)	Rear Suspension	Live axle on half-elliptic leaf springs, lever-arm dampers
Engine Size	3,528cc		
Engine Format	V-8	Tires	175 HR 14 radial
Carburetion	2 × SU HIF6	Brakes	Lockheed brakes, Front 10.7-in (27.2 cm) discs; rear 10.175-in (25.85 cm) drums, vacuum servo assistance
Max Bhp	137 bhp @ 5,000 rpm		
Max Torque	193 lb-ft @ 2,900 rpm		
		0 to 60 mph	8.6 sec
		Top Speed	124 mph (199.56 km/h)
		Fuel Economy	23.4 mpg (US, 19.48 mpg)

1974–1976
As above for 1974–1976 polyeurethane-bumper model, except

Models	Coupe (£1,925 to £3,317)
Length	158.25 in (401.96 cm)
Height	51 in (129.5 cm)

CHAPTER 12

REBIRTH:

RV8, MGF, ET AL

Lamenting the demise of MG, aficionados' hopes rose with development of the RV8 using British Motor Heritage bodies and the Buick-sourced V-8. The genesis, design, and construction of the all-new MGF saw a new look for MG take root. Other models, such as the wild Group B homologation special 6R4, returned to the competition front. But a final new owner and line-up spelled the end.

This MG ZR's refurbishment of standard Rover fare successfully endowed the vehicles with an aggressive aesthetic. Performance tweaking helped to mask the by-now-aging underpinnings.

After a 1980 prototype Aston Martin MGB—produced by a possible takeover consortium—proved to be a dead end, it looked as if the MG brand would fade into oblivion just as many other famous British marques had done. Over in the US, franchise dealers were despairing for news of a new MG sports car, but it soon became clear that this was a nonstarter.

However, in May 1982 green shoots appeared in the shape of the new MG Metro. Built at Longbridge, the former Austin factory just south of Birmingham, it was a sportier version of the standard Austin Mini Metro hatchback. This was familiar ground for MG, as its transversely mounted engine/front-wheel-drive layout suspension harked back to the MG1100 and 1300s of the late sixties and early seventies.

Rather than distinctly badge-engineered, this version wore the MG name—and all the associations of its considerable sporting heritage—as an adornment. To be fair, it wasn't all cosmetic. Alongside larger 12.4 inch (315 mm) metric alloy wheels, low-profile tires, a rear spoiler, and a tweaked interior (with red carpets and seatbelts), performance *was* improved. The 1,275cc A-Plus engine, which received a healthy 12-brake-horsepower increase (and without a second carburetor in sight!) to 72 bhp, was now capable of 100-miles-per-hour (161 km/h) performance.

Even in much reduced form MG was, as a brand, back on the main stage.

1982–1991

By 1982, BLMC's new name—Austin Rover Group— excised the company from the impression of corporate incompetence that came from any association with British Leyland and its various forms.

(Left) MG Maestro 1600 featured an electronic dashboard and a synthesized voice that instructed and warned the driver. Neither caught on.

(Opposite) From the depths of despair to a rebirth of sorts, the famous octagon made a comeback on the hatchback MG Metro.

The MG Metro Turbo arrived hot on the MG Metro's heels endowed with a significant leap in performance. Its strengthened low-compression engine, still carburetor-fed but now joined by a Garrett T3 turbocharger, was capable of 93 brake horsepower; bigger brakes, stiffer suspension, and, once again, wider 5.5J 13-inch alloy wheels joined it. Unlike most of this new generation of turbocharged cars that, once the turbocharger had spooled up, delivered their power in an almighty spurt, it did so smoothly and consistently through the rev range.

It'd be nice to say that this was entirely by design, but the reality was that the Lotus engineers involved in its development had dialed down the boost to protect the antiquated transmission (which still had only four cogs). Still *Motor Sport* called it, "a great little fun carriage" and praised both its handling and smooth acceleration. The Turbo continued in production until 1990 (gaining in 1987–1988 strange "floating octagon" decals—for cost

saving it was a single decal, split and applied to both sides so the front of one side was the rear of the other), selling 21,968 examples.

Next up the following year was the MG Maestro, with innovative but short-lived electronic fascia and voice synthesizer. Its first incarnation had a 102 brake horsepower, 1600 R-Series engine, but ARG quickly replaced that with the more reliable 115 brake horsepower S-Series unit.

The three-box MG Montego 2.0EFi sedan arrived in 1984, as did its sibling, the MG Maestro 2.0EFi. Cynics of earlier badge-engineering products (originally instigated by BMC) gladly noted that modern MGs were now also differentiated from their standard brethren by the incorporation of red bumper stripes, seat belts, instrument graphics, and upholstery trim.

Unlike the MG Metro Turbo, the MG Montego Turbo of 1985 was a tire-scrabbling hooligan of a beast. Despite

A hooligan in sedan clothes, the MG Montego Turbo was an unruly brute that struggled to lay down its considerable power through the front wheels.

heavily modified suspension, with 150 brake horsepower trying to escape the front wheels early versions quickly gained a reputation for unstable road holding—even far from approaching the limit—although this did improve somewhat on later versions.

The arrival of the exotic-looking (and sounding) EX-E prototype, with its plastic-panel-clothed aluminum alloy frame and 6R4 V-6 specified power plant, at that year's Frankfurt Motor Show briefly titillated the MG public—until it became clear that its chances of going into production were exactly nil.

Austin Rover became the Rover Group in 1986, and two years later its "British Motor Heritage" subsidiary began producing replacement MGB Roadster bodies, using the original factory pressings, for enthusiast restorers. The corporate front was once again in upheaval over a new owner: British Aerospace.

British Aerospace oversaw the final MG product of that era, the £12,999 MG Maestro Turbo. Heavily

revised suspension meant this road-burner was better developed than its Montego brethren but, with the same engine producing 152 brake horsepower, equally capable on the performance front. Styling embellishment from a Tickford-designed body kit, though, was less than

Power rose to a heady 93 bhp in the MG Metro Turbo, but unlike most period turbocharged cars, output was a slow-burner in order to protect the gearbox.

MG METRO 6R4

In February 1984, Austin Rover Motorsport unveiled an ambitious project, undertaken in conjunction with Williams Grand Prix Engineering. Designed to take on the titans of Group B rallying—including Lancia, Audi, and Peugeot—the MG Metro 6R4 rally car visually resembled the production Mini Metro, even though it included just sixteen standard panels. Under the skin, however, it was an entirely bespoke, high-performance weapon.

The seam-welded tubular chassis featured a built-in roll cage. A mid-mounted, all-alloy, compact 3-liter, Quad-Cam 24-valve V-6 engine with a Cosworth-produced cylinder head and internals provided power. Ahead of this and mated to it, the Williams-designed gearbox drove all four wheels via a Ferguson Formula viscous coupling. Power output for the full rally spec cars was 410 brake horsepower, but even the road-going "Clubman" spec (200 were constructed for homologation purposes) still had a mighty, for the time, 250 brake horsepower.

It performed extraordinarily well on its debut, with Tony Pond setting nine fastest stage times and finishing third overall on the November 1985 Lombard-RAC Rally. Subsequent outings

weren't quite as spectacular, and it quickly became apparent the vehicle was underpowered compared to opposing cars, which were now approaching the 600 brake horsepower mark.

In 1986, after a series of horrendous, high-profile accidents resulting in the deaths of both drivers and spectators, the motorsport governing body Fédération Internationale du Sport Automobile (FISA) pulled the Group B category completely. With no class in which its car could compete, and already dismayed by ever-spiraling costs, Austin Rover followed suit and ended the program.

Adding to the disappointment, many of the "Clubman" cars remained unsold, although they went on to be popular in the 300 brake horsepower–limited British National Rally series. Despite tapping the MG name, the reality was that, just like their production car equivalents, the rally cars had little to do with the marque.

If there's any consolation, perhaps it's that Kimber, in his 1930s pomp (purpose-built K3 Magnette, Q-Type and R-Type Midget racers, and all), no doubt would have appreciated the team's considerable attention to bespoke design detail.

Pond powers his MG Metro 6R4 to an impressive 3rd-place finish on the 1985 Lombard-RAC Rally, setting nine fastest stage times to boot.

subtle. Capable of 0 to 60 miles per hour in 6.9 seconds and a top speed of 129 miles per hour (208 km/h), for its time it was the quickest hatchback in the UK and a rapid means of transporting four people.

The company built just 501 before ceasing MG production in 1991 to concentrate on the arrival of the new Rover models.

1992–1994: RETURN OF THE ROADSTER

The new MG sports car displayed at the 1992 Birmingham Motor Show leaned heavily into retro. David Bishop, managing director of British Motor Heritage, instigated

the venture with his musings on the achievability of an updated nineties MGB using a Heritage body shell. Rover's Special Projects Team subsequently took up the concept, and Project Adder was born.

Constructed using traditional hand-built assembly methods in a corner of Rover's Cowley plant (the same former Pressed Steel factory that once supplied Morris Motors), the final production car body retained only 25 percent of its claimed MGB ancestry: the floorpan, doors, and trunk lid. The team remodeled the rest for a fresh, updated look that included body-colored bumpers, sills, a longer nose, and wider arches under which sat 15-inch (38.1 cm) alloy wheels sporting 205/65 profile tires.

(Above) This rear three-quarter shot shows a nicely resolved design. The body was based on an MGB heritage shell, but the hand-build process saw almost every panel reshaped.

(Left) Beautifully finished with lashings of leather and wood veneer in a traditional style, the RV8's interior was a resounding success.

(Opposite) The MG Maestro Turbo was a more successful high-performance sedan, capable of transporting four adults at high speed. Its Tickford body kit was less than subtle, though.

Meanwhile, under the hood sat the Dorian Gray of engines, Rover's ubiquitous V-8; now, after more than three decades' development, in 3.9-liter 190 brake horsepower fuel-injected form. The transmission was a five-speed unit originally seen in the Rover SD1. The braking system had ventilated discs at the front but drums at the rear, while the rear axle was a big and beefy solid unit with no limited-slip differential. They completed this mix and match of new and old with suspension partly of a bygone—featuring half-elliptic leaf springs—but with modern telescopic shock absorbers, anti-sway bars, and rear torque-control arms.

The high-quality finish of a cabin that included beautiful stone-colored leather seats and a polished elm veneer dashboard and door cappings, as well as the stunning exterior paint endowed by Cowley's modern finishing processes, stood out immediately.

Guidance notes issued to the press by the Rover Group outlined the concept: "to recreate a classic British sports car/ to celebrate the 30th anniversary of the MGB/ a delight to own and drive/ a car for enthusiasts/ a classic car without drawbacks." Two points also included in the document, "takes the risk out of buying an old car" and "full Rover warranties including corrosion," added sound logical arguments on key points that affected most classic-car owners. A new open-topped, two-seater MG sports car already provided an emotional pull. The only fly in the ointment was the price; at £25,440 (£26,500 at launch), it was an exceedingly pricey car.

The Rover Group made it clear that this was a limited-run production for the home market only, in right-hand-drive form only—a fact bemoaned in a preview by US-based *Road & Track*.

The return of the octagon to the sports car arena was big news, and on its release the UK motoring press quickly cleared their front pages to make way for the RV8. In its June 1993 road test, the recently merged *Autocar & Motor* gave performance four stars—0 to 60 miles per hour in 5.9 seconds (allegedly) and 135 miles per hour (216.7 km/h) were not to be sniffed at—and generally liked its appearance. But the article didn't hold back on its opinion of the ride and handling: "Try to bully the RV8 along, and the entire gamut of horrors from terminal understeer to roll oversteer will unfold before you." There was no masking the fact that, despite being modified, its leaf-sprung, solid axle rear end was hopelessly out of date. As such, overall, it gained two stars, with the caveat, "it is easy to enjoy and even fun to drive in an agricultural, vintage manner. If, however, you asked us whether we would part with £25,440 for the pleasure of its company, we would regretfully have to decline."

Others, such as P*erformance Car*, were a little more forgiving and appreciative of the siginificant efforts that had gone into producing the RV8. However, the much-anticipated sales to UK MG enthusiasts failed to materialize in the numbers expected. At £24,803, a base spec TVR Griffith 4.0 was cheaper, significantly faster, and had a more sophisticated suspension setup.

Japan became the hope on the horizon. Despite their statements to the contrary, The Rover Group considered changing their UK-only stance as far back as late 1991, signing off on "Adder Phase 2—MG RV8 Japan" on August

British Motor Heritage's construction of MGB Heritage bodyshells led directly to the birth of a modern take on the classic model.

19, 1993. Japanese-market cars had air-conditioning, a catalyst overheat warning system, and wheelarch flares (both legal requirements), as well as "Rover" script badges on the side of each front fender.

The decision to move forward proved prescient. The reaction of both the Japanese public and press to the car at the 1993 Tokyo Motor Show was marvelous. Of the 2000 produced, a staggering 1,568 headed to the Far East.

Today there's no doubt that the RV8 is a handsome looking, modern take on the original MGB—the V8 roadster that the UK never got back in the 1970s. It's nicely finished, has power to spare, and in a straight line remains a consummate GT. Its successful retro design predated the Volkswagen Beetle, BMW Mini, and Fiat 500, showing their respective designers the way forward.

Yes, it had its flaws in period—certainly more forgivable today for any prospective buyer of this modern classic—for some its lack of modern niceties, such as power steering, ABS, and air conditioning, were too much to stomach. But it did exactly what it was designed to do and succeeded in bringing MG back into the sports car consciousness.

It was, in fact, merely an aperitif for what was to follow.

1995–2000: A PROPER RETURN

In yet another—and not the last—change of ownership, MG and its fellows in the company found themselves in BMW's hands in 1994, to the tune of £800 million. Though some lamented the "loss" of two famous British marques, if anyone could get value out of the MG name then surely it was the ladies and gentlemen of Munich.

(Left) This interior features that scourge of modern vehicles: a mountain of dark gray plastic; here it's broken up by wooden inserts and the standard cream-faced instrument dials.

(Below) The high rear end of the MGF was well resolved and, in original non-spoiler form, looks particularly clean.

(Opposite) The frontal view shows just how smart McGovern's design is—unmistakably MG but at the same time both modern and dynamic.

The marque could have had a mid-engined car in its line-up as far back as the early seventies. The ADO21 Austin-Morris and MG prototypes pursuing exactly this layout (the MG would have no doubt wore an "MGD" badge) were unceremoniously discarded thanks to the overt Triumph bias within the upper echelons of British Leyland at the time.

Beginning in 1989, the Rover Group investigated five possible routes, covering various engine positions, driven wheels, body designs and panels, and target audiences, for a new MG sports car. "Project Phoenix" was derived from this process. They eventually chose PR3, the mid-engined/rear-wheel-drive route, and developed it alongside the RV8.

The Rover Group's Canley Design Studio under Gerry McGovern further refined the concept, designing a simple but strong steel monocoque chassis. Its short nose/high tail styling, indicative of its engine's mid/transverse placement, featured an agreeable and rounded modern style—not overtly aggressive, but with just enough sporting intent. The studio raided the existing Rover hatchback model range for the running gear. The decision to use the aluminum Rover K-Series unit in a larger 1,796cc form and mate it to a Rover 200/400 gearbox was a no-brainer, as the twin overhead camshaft design had exactly the free-revving nature required. All-independent Moulton Hydrogas suspension came from the Rover 100, with modified Metro/Rover 100 subframes providing mounting points for double wishbones. To this they added modern telescopic shock absorbers and four-wheel disc brakes, and, having learned from the RV8, included electric power-assisted steering and anti-lock brakes as standard (and air conditioning, an optional extra) on the higher-spec model.

The Rover Group made an agreement with Mayflower of Coventry, who invested in the necessary tooling for body production at its Motor Panels plant in return for a profit share, and set up an MG Cars subsidiary to handle sales of the new model. Then the change in company ownership put everything on hold, and those involved in Project Phoenix held their collective breaths. . .

Despite its considerable development progress, the new model had no guarantee of approval from BMW. Thankfully, the new boss gave the green light, and the marque was back. Assembled in Longbridge—Abingdon was a distant memory—the first all-new MG sports car since the MGB in 1962 was on its way.

The vehicle revealed at the 1995 Geneva Motor Show was just what the MG faithful had been wanting for so long: smart looks, excellent build quality, a punchy base engine (with an even more powerful option), a pliant ride, and, underlying it all, that sporting MG character. And, unlike the RV8, its pricing was spot on: £15.995 for the basic 118 brake horsepower 1.8i (capable of 0 to 60 miles per hour in 8.7 seconds and a 120 miles per hour top speed) and £17,995 for the up-rated 143 brake horsepower variable valve control (VVC) model (capable of 0 to 60 miles per hour in 7.6 seconds and a 130 miles per hour top speed).

In the October issue, *Car* magazine journalist Gavin Green put the entry-level model up against the new Fiat Barchetta, Alfa Romeo Spider, and the car that had single-handedly redefined and regenerated the genre, the Mazda MX-5. Of the MGF's aesthetics, he could hardly have been more positive. "The MG is the most modern—a neat design with a terrific, chunky, no flab posture, like a muscle-bound terrier."

However, it was the car's handling that shone. Alluding to most mid-engined vehicles' propensity for quickly swapping ends at the limits of adhesion, he said, "Not the MGF. This car feels planted on the track, and it stays utterly neutral. Its grip is terrific, yet it isn't so unerring that you can't tidy its trajectory with your right foot." He continued to praise its "clever design and brilliantly complete engineering." A front cover dominated by the words "MGF-ing marvellous!" accompanied these glowing words.

Car magazine's October 1995 front cover left readers in no doubt as to its thoughts on MG's newcomer.

BACK ON THE RECORD TRAIL

Californian Land Rover technician, and experienced Bonneville Salt Flats driver, Kilbourne is at the wheel of EXF (later known as EX253) on its way to a record-breaking top speed run of 217.4 mph (348.35 kph).

After a 38–year gap, MG returned to the record car trail in September 1997. This was thanks to MG Metro 6R4 project engineer Wynne Mitchell, who had pitched the initial concept and gotten the go-ahead from senior management.

Mitchell based the EX-F (later known as EX-253) on a standard MGF. Constructed at Rover's Gaydon facility, its David Woodhouse-designed body remained recognizably MGF in profile, but with the addition of a tapered tail, flat-deck tonneau cover, a teardrop driver's canopy, and a roll bar. The project relied heavily on racing and rally driver Tony Pond during the development and proving stages of the turbocharged 1.4-liter Janspeed-tuned engine.

The company chose Terry Kilbourne, a Californian Land Rover technician with significant Bonneville experience, to be the prototype's driver, shipping the whole ensemble to the States. Final tweaks actually took place on the driveway of Kilbourne's home before the team set off for the Salt Flats of Utah.

There Kilbourne took MG back into the record books as he piloted the 329-brake-horsepower EX253, complete with lightning bolt on its exterior (a nod to the Gardner-MG), to a speed of 217.4 mph (348.35 km/h).

Buoyed by this success and the resultant publicity, BMW hatched an even more ambitious plan for the following year: to top Phil Hill's 1951 record of 254.9 mph (409.2 km/h) achieved in EX181—and perhaps even break the 300-mph mark. The team set to work again, constructing the EX255, bringing RAF pilot Andy Green—who'd broken the land speed record in Thrust SSC—on board.

Alas, there was no fairytale ending. With a 942-brake-horsepower twin-supercharged MG-developed V-8, the record car's prowess wasn't in doubt. However, in the build-up to the record runs at the 50th Bonneville Speed Week, it suffered a leak from the hydraulic clutch slave cylinder, and the attempt had to be abandoned.

It seems the Great British public agreed, and by the end of 1996—its first full production year—the MGF supplanted the MX-5 to become the UK's best-selling sports car. In December, *Autocar*'s Allan Muir had only positive things to report on living with a VVC-engine endowed MGF for 10,000 miles, with its "all-new design with a pukka mid-engined layout, a terrifically rigid chassis, rear-wheel-drive and state of the art engines." His only complaint was the inefficient heating and ventilation system. As a starter, it was a remarkably positive introduction.

An MGF Abingdon LE special edition arrived in spring of 1998, finished in a unique nonmetallic Brooklands Green and with accoutrements that included chrome door handles, polished stainless-steel grilles, and 16-inch (41 cm) alloy wheels. BMW also built an interesting Super Sports concept car for that year's Geneva Motor Show.

In 1999 the company commissioned a second special edition, the MGF 75 LE, to celebrate 75(-ish) years of MG. Again, the major difference was in body color and, in this case, hood color, as well as a chrome theme and special badges.

Of more interest perhaps was the introduction in 2000 of the new Steptronic CVT gearbox option, a new clutchless transmission with shifts operated either by a traditional gear selector or steering wheel-mounted buttons; it didn't however prove to be a great seller. At the same time, the MGF range received a minor facelift that included trim changes and color additions.

A Wedgewood special edition followed in July 2000, complete with a unique silver-blue hue and, for the first time, a spoiler.

However, just as it ever was, nothing stood still in the MG world, and changes were afoot once more.

2001–2005: A FALSE SAVIOR

Despite the success of the MGF, BMW tired of trying to make the Rover brand turn a profit and put the company up for sale. Of two potential saviors (the other being a British venture capital company called Alchemy Partners), The Phoenix Group won out and paid the princely sum of just £10 to the German manufacturer, which cast it adrift with £75 million (in lieu of warranties) and an interest free, 49-year loan of £427 million.

The future seemed assured and exciting. Quickly renamed the MG Rover Group, it got to work on refreshing the MGF. A base model 1.6i offered 111 brake horsepower, the 1.8i continued as is, and, at the top end, the new "Trophy" boasted 158 brake horsepower with 0 to 60 miles per hour dipping below 7 seconds (only just, at 6.9 seconds) for the first time. The MG Rover Group

MGF TROPHY 160 SE

RGS-0101-001

An MG Rover Group Communications (++ 44 (0)121 781 8491) photograph. Copyright free for editorial purposes, not for unauthorised resale. For any other use, prior written permission is required.

Top-spec MGF Trophy 160SE was introduced by the MG Rover Group, as was a base-level 1.6i model.

SUPERCAR AMBITIONS

MG Rover, struggling to make a profit and in decline, took a seemingly crazy chance and embarked upon one last flight of fancy by buying Qvale Automotive. Among its new acquisition's models was the Ford V-8–powered Mangusta, a front-engined, rear-wheel-drive super car, and management intended to build an MG aimed firmly at the supercar market.

MG Rover's purchase of Qvale allowed it to shortcut the lengthy development process that a new model necessitated, but it quickly scrapped its original conservatively styled MG X80 concept (gone was the Mangusta's retractable hard-top, for it was now a coupe).

Instead, after more work, they settled on a new wild-looking, predominantly carbon-fiber body-shell. Penned by design director Peter Stevens, it had huge, muscular arches; "shark-gill" front fender air outlets; a Kamm tail-style rear end; and a big, blunt front-end. Subtle it was not. Power came via the tried-and-tested Ford V-8, similar to that fitted in the ZT 260 V-8.

At its October 2002 preview, MG gained just 29 advance orders. The asking prices—£65,000 for the now renamed entry-level X Power SV and £83,000 SV-R—no doubt put many off a model from a brand that had no previous supercar record.

The production process itself was convoluted, with shells constructed in Turin and mechanical assembly, with the engine and transmission flown in from Detroit, taking place in Modena before cars traveled to Great Britain for painting, trimming, and road testing prior to sale.

If the company's plan appeared flawed (low construction numbers meant it stood little chance of being profitable), one thing that couldn't be denied was the performance, which was epic. With 320–402 brake horsepower available, it was a rumbling V-8 bad boy, and in top spec it was capable of sprinting from 0 to 60 mph in under 5 seconds.

Unfortunately the buying public remained unconvinced. Despite its considerable abilities, this MG supercar's draw was negligible.

The MG supercar project in its ultimate SV-R form fought the dying of the flame. Despite formidable performance abilities and wild aesthetics, there was very little appetite for it.

If the later SV-R was folly, then the ZT 260 and ZT-T 260 weren't far behind. There's no doubt they were brutal and effective road burners but converting the standard models to rear-wheel drive didn't come cheap.

offered it in new colors, Trophy Yellow and Trophy Blue (as well as the existing Solar Red and Black), and it had unique, 16-inch (41 cm) alloy wheels, four-pot AP racing front-brake calipers, new front and rear spoilers, a black headlight finish, and body-colored interior trim panels.

To generate positive publicity for the marque it was time to resume racing (the one make MGF Cup Championship race series had run since 1998 and would be superseded in 2005 by the MG Trophy Championship), and for a return to one particular French track. In April 2001 the company formed MG Sport & Racing Ltd (alongside the sub-brand "MG X Power") to oversee this.

With BMW gone, the MG badge could now also be applied to sporting sedans, hatchbacks, and estate models. The Phoenix Group targeted the Rover 25, 45, and 75. Initial X-designations quickly gave way to Z. The MG ZR, ZS, ZT, and ZT-T estate quickly came to market, each with painted radiator shells as part of design director Peter Stevens' successful (if a tad boy-racerish) visual updates. While power outputs were pretty potent, there was no disguising the fact that by now some the base products (certainly the Rover 25 and 45) were old technology.

In January 2002, the new MG TF replaced the MGF. Again, it had a restyled, marginally more aggressive exterior that featured a modified version of the Le Mans EX257's four-aperture nose box. The biggest technology change was the introduction of multilink independent rear suspension and coil springs over telescopic dampers to replace its predecessor's Hydragas setup. The resultant stirring handling was a boon to a model still selling around 15,000 units per year.

The MG TF took its styling cues from the Le Mans racer, with its distinctive four aperture "nostrils" and central octagon badge.

A LE MANS RETURN

The company joined forces with Lola Cars for its return to Le Mans. A lack of engine development hampered its chances at the French track, but EX257 later proved hugely successful in US Prototype Racing series. A separate British Touring Cars program was not a success.

Piggybacking on its successful Nissan-engined B2K/40 LMP625–class prototype racer, MG joined forces with Lola Cars International Ltd for an emotional return to Le Mans in 2001. Together they constructed the new MGB01/60 model (codenamed EX257) using all the main design elements from the car that had finished 29th at the 2000 event, winning the LMP625 category.

Incorporating a small nose-cone box wearing the famous octagon made it identifiably MG, as did luminous green decals set against the cars' black finish. The engine, though, was a problem.

Unwilling to put its name on a car with someone else's engine, the group pulled the Nissan unit in favor of an Advanced Engine Research (AER)—developed one based on MG's own XP20 2.0-liter turbocharged 4-cylinder design. With a proven chassis and a power output of 500 brake horsepower in a lightweight car (1,521.2 lb [690 kg]) that lent it an excellent power-to-weight ratio, this should have been a match made in heaven.

In 2001 the entered cars qualified 14th and 17th overall and best in class, with lap times perturbing even the dominant Audis in the bigger LMP900 category. Unfortunately the engine's rushed development (it'd only been running for a month) meant both highly stressed units failed.

They returned the following year, after yet more engine development, and qualified 6th and 12th. Reliability was better, with both cars lasting well into the night, but ultimately, they were still unable to finish. At this point MG Rover pulled its funding. Intersport Racing entered a single car in 2003, but it, too, failed to finish.

Lola, in conjunction with AER, continued to develop and sell the EX257. It eventually proved its worth in the American Le Mans Series, when Dyson Racing Team won the 2003 LMP675 championship. Pitted against Audi R8 teams in the full LMP1 category in 2004 and 2005, Dyson finished runners-up both times and the EX257 scored some notable individual victories.

Despite BMW's largesse on departure, development money was desperately tight. There were two attempts to jazz up the model range. In 2003, the ZT 260 and ZT-T 260 received Ford's 4.6-liter SOHC V-8 engine (from the contemporary Mustang), a Tremec manual gearbox, and Hydratrak limited-slip differential. With 260 brake horsepower, these comprehensively reengineered cars (now rear-wheel-drive) could power from 0 to 60 miles per hour in 6.2 seconds on their way to a top speed of 155 miles per hour. These were brutal, capable, and thirsty (20 miles per gallon) cars, but at £30,000 never destined to be best sellers.

The second such effort, that same year, took the marque deep into unchartered territory.

The ZR and ZS received facelifts for 2004, and the TF gained a slightly more compliant suspension setup. However, having one successful model was never going to sustain the company (even one with just one factory), and, with meek production levels elsewhere, an aging model range, and a chronic lack of development funds, it was clear that MG Rover's time, like that of its predecessors, was coming to an end.

When last-minute talks with state-owned Shanghai Automotive Industry Corporation (SAIC) of China collapsed, MG Rover filed for bankruptcy on the 7th of April, 2005. After 81 years, some incredibly successful cars—others less so—and many different owners, manufacture of the famous octagon ceased for the last time.

As their names suggest, shoehorning a Ford V-8 into the ZT 260 and ZT-T 260's engine bays was good for a beastly 260 bhp.

1992-1994

RV8

Models	Two-Seater Roadster (£26,500)	Gearbox	5-speed manual
Construction	Steel monocoque structure	Automatic	n/a
Length	158 in (401 cm)	Final Drive Ratio	3.31:1
Width	67 in (169.4 cm)	Steering	Rack and pinion
Height	52 in (132 cm)	Front Suspension	Independent with double wishbone, coil springs, telescopic dampers, anti-roll bar
Wheelbase	92 in (233 cm)		
Weight	2,822 lb (1,280 kg)	Rear Suspension	Live axle with control arms, tapered leaf semi-elliptic springs, telescopic dampers, anti-roll bar
Engine Size	3,946cc		
Engine Format	V-8		
Carburetion	Lucas multipoint fuel injection	Tires	6 x 15 in
Max Bhp	187 bhp @ 4,750 rpm	Breaks	11 in (28 cm) disc brakes, front; drums, rear
Max Torque	231 lb-ft @ 3,200 rpm		
		0 To 60 mph	5.9 sec (Rover estimate)
		Top Speed	135 mph (216.7 km/h)
		Fuel Economy	20.2 mpg (US, 16.8 mpg)

1995

MGF 1.8i

Models	Two-seater Roadster (£15,995)	Gearbox	5-speed manual
Construction	Steel monocoque	Automatic	n/a
Length	154.1 in (391.4 cm)	Final Drive Ratio	3.938:1
Width	64.1 in (162.8 cm)	Steering	Rack and pinion (optional PAS)
Height	49.6 in (126 cm)	Front Suspension	Independent with double wishbone, interconnected Hydragas springs, anti-roll bar
Wheelbase	93.7 in (238 cm)		
Weight	2,337 lb (1,060 kg)	Rear Suspension	Independent with double wishbone, interconnected Hydragas springs, anti-roll bar
Engine Size	1,796cc		
Engine Format	In-line 4-cylinder		
Carburetion	Multipoint fuel injection	Tires	6 x 15 in
Max Bhp	118 bhp @ 5,500 rpm	Brakes	9.5-in (24.1 cm) ventilated disc brakes, front; solid, rear
Max Torque	122 lb ft @ 3,000 rpm		
		0 to 60 mph	8.5 sec
		Top Speed	120 mph (193 km/h)
		Fuel Economy	38.3 mpg (US, 31.9 mpg)

1995-2000

MGF 1.8i VVC, as above, except

Models	Two-seater Roadster (£18,875)	Gearbox	5-speed manual (optional Steptronic from 2000)
Max Bhp	143 bhp @ 7,000 rpm		
Max Torque	130 lb ft @ 3,000 rpm	Final Drive Ratio	4.2:1
		0 to 60 mph	7.0 sec
		Top Speed	130 mph (209 km/h)

2001

MGF 1.6i as above, except

Models	Two-seater Roadster (£15,335)	**Brakes**	9.5-in (24.1 cm) ventilated disc brakes, front; solid, rear; ABS
Max Bhp	111 @ 6,250 rpm		
Max Torque	107 lb ft @ 4,700 rpm	**0 to 60 mph**	9.6 sec
Gearbox	5-speed manual	**Top Speed**	116 mph (187 km/h)
Final Drive Ratio	3.938:1	**Fuel Economy**	38.4 mpg (US, 32 mpg)

2001

MGF Trophy as above, except

Models	Two-seater Roadster (£20,815)	**Brakes**	11.9-in (30.4 cm) ventilated disc brakes, front; solid, rear; ABS
Max Bhp	158 bhp @ 7,000 rpm		
Max Torque	128 lb ft @ 4,500 rpm	**0 to 60 mph**	6.9 sec
Gearbox	5-speed manual	**Top Speed**	137 mph (220.5 km/h)
Final Drive Ratio	4.2:1	**Fuel Economy**	36.3 mpg (US, 30.2 mpg)

2001

MGF 1.8i as above, except

Models	Two-seater Roadster (£16,851)	**Breaks**	9.5-in (24.1 cm) ventilated disc brakes, front; solid, rear; ABS
Max Bhp	119 bhp @ 5,500 rpm		
Max Torque	121 lb-ft @ 3,000 rpm	**0 To 60 mph**	10.4 sec
Gearbox	5-speed manul	**Top Speed**	120 mph (198 km/h)
Final Drive Ratio	3.938:1	**Fuel Economy**	38.4 mpg (US, 32 mpg)

2001

MGTF 1.8VVC as above, except

Models	Two-seater Roadster (£19,315); Trophy (£20,815)	**Final Drive Ratio**	4.05:1
Max Bhp	143 bhp @ 7,000 rpm	**Breaks**	11.9-in (30.4 cm) ventilated disc brakes, front; solid, rear; ABS
Max Torque	128 lb-ft @ 4,500 rpm	**0 To 60 mph**	7.6 sec
Gearbox	5-speed manual (optional ZF 6-speed sequential)	**Top Speed**	130 mph (209 km/h)
		Fuel Economy	36.3 mpg (US, 30.2 mpg)

(Right) Built in China, shipped to the UK, and then assembled at Longbridge, the 2008 limited edition TF LE 500 kickstarted MG sales in its former home.

(Below) Unveiled in Mumbai on May 15, 2019, the hybrid Hector SUV is the company's first foray into the Indian market.

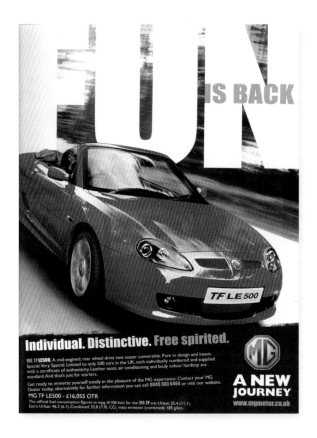

Except of course, it didn't.

Nanjing Automobile bought the name and manufacturing rights in July 2005, dismantled the Longbridge production lines, shipped them to China, and reassembled them there.

The first Chinese-built, Chinese-market MG TFs appeared in 2007 with assembly of a special UK-market TF LE500 model—using imported components—symbolically taking place at Longbridge the following year.

MG's new owner merged with SAIC in 2008, and the first all-new model, the five-door MG6 hatchback, appeared in 2011. A four-door saloon followed in 2012, once again wearing famous "Magnette" designation, it won the manufacturer's title for the 2014 British Touring Car Championship.

Today MG Motor in Longbridge conceives its models, which continue to be built in China. Brand ethos is based firmly on value for money. As I write this, it is the UK's fastest-growing car manufacturer, with more than 100 dealers (and growing).

It released its latest products, the compact crossover MG HS and an all-electric MG EV, to decent reviews. If you think the idea of an MG-badged SUV faintly ridiculous, then so too is the thought of one from Alfa Romeo, Bentley, Rolls-Royce, Lamborghini, Aston Martin . . . the list goes on.

The hope is that as the company continues to find its feet and goes from strength to strength financially, it will begin to look further back for inspiration.

Despite a modern market dominated by SUVs, perhaps there still remains room for a smartly styled, octagon-wearing, two-seater sports car; one that is based on existing running gear, highly affordable, and endowed with a certain type of sporting character.

Now wouldn't that be something?

ACKNOWLEDGMENTS

It's been an absolute pleasure to immerse myself in the world of MG sports cars for the last twelve months, and there are several people I'd like to thank for their help in producing this book.

First and foremost, all the ladies in my life, including my wife Angela, daughter Genevieve, and mother Jasmine. You kept me grounded at all times, and your collective good humor (and sharp tongues) ensured that I never got too big for my proverbial boots. For that very same reason, I'd also like to thank my father Talib, and brothers Lee and Ben.

My editor Dennis Pernu has been patient, focused, and always ready to offer sage advice whenever necessary. I'd like to express my gratitude to him and also thank the rest of the Motorbooks team, including project manager Jessi Schatz and copy editor Andrea Zander, for their professionalism.

Christopher Keevill and Rodney Kettel at the Early M.G. Society helped immeasurably in my understanding of both the marque's origins and its early offerings.

The feedback and observations of the MG Car Club's various individual model registers have also been invaluable. As such, I'd like to thank the Triple M Register, the SVW Register, the T Register, the Y Register, the Magnette Register, the MGA Register, the Midget Register, the MGB Register, the MGC Register, the V8 Register (also for pointing me in the direction of both Don Hayter's 2002 talk to members and *Sports Car World's* 1967 article), the FWD Register, and the MGF Register.

I'd also like to express my gratitude to Dick Morbey, Peter Green, Garry Perry, Chris Callaghan, Peter Vielvoye, Neil Cairns, Paul Batho, Ian Wilson, Mike Authers, John Watson, Colin Howes, Jim Lott, Nigel May, Keith Williams, Keith Belcher, and Damon Milnes.

Finally I'd like to give thanks to the following for supplying pictures: Celia Palmer, the Early M.G. Society, Nicolas Lecompte, Colin Howes, Neil Cairns, Tristan Judge and photographer Angus Taylor at online UK auction house the Market (themarket.co.uk), James Mann, Simon Clay, and Simon Percival at the Percival Motor Company (percivalmotorco.co.uk).

PHOTO CREDITS

Inspiring | Educating | Creating | Entertaining

Brimming with creative inspiration, how-to projects, and useful information to enrich your everyday life, Quarto Knows is a favorite destination for those pursuing their interests and passions. Visit our site and dig deeper with our books into your area of interest: Quarto Creates, Quarto Cooks, Quarto Homes, Quarto Lives, Quarto Drives, Quarto Explores, Quarto Gifts, or Quarto Kids.

First Published in 2020 by Motorbooks, an imprint of The Quarto Group, 100 Cummings Center, Suite 265-D, Beverly, MA 01915, USA. T (978) 282-9590 F (978) 283-2742 QuartoKnows.com

Motorbooks titles are also available at discount for retail, wholesale, promotional, and bulk purchase. For details, contact the Special Sales Manager by email at specialsales@quarto.com or by mail at The Quarto Group, Attn: Special Sales Manager, 100 Cummings Center, Suite 265-D, Beverly, MA 01915, USA.

24 23 22 21 20   1 2 3 4 5

ISBN: 978-0-7603-6717-9

Digital edition published in 2020
eISBN: 978-0-7603-6718-6

Library of Congress Cataloging-in-Publication Data

Names: Alkureishi, Ross, author.
Title: The complete book of classic MG cars / Ross Alkureishi.
Description: Beverly, MA, USA : Motorbooks, 2020. | Includes index.
Identifiers: LCCN 2020023561 (print) | LCCN 2020023562 (ebook) |
 ISBN 9780760367179 (hardcover) | ISBN 9780760367186 (ebook)
Subjects: LCSH: M.G. automobiles.
Classification: LCC TL215.M2 A39 2020 (print) | LCC TL215.M2 (ebook) |
 DDC 629.222--dc23
LC record available at https://lccn.loc.gov/2020023561
LC ebook record available at https://lccn.loc.gov/2020023562

Acquiring Editor: Dennis Pernu
Cover Image: James Mann
Cover and book design: Landers Miller Design

Printed in China